TABLE OF CONTENTS

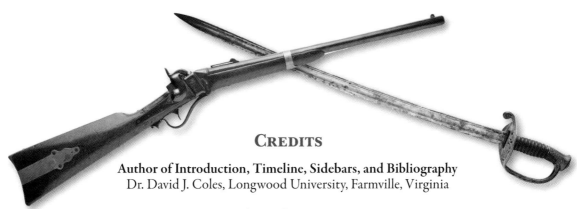

CREDITS

Author of Introduction, Timeline, Sidebars, and Bibliography
Dr. David J. Coles, Longwood University, Farmville, Virginia

Authors of Site Entries
Frederick P. Gaske, Historic Preservation Services,
and David Stanford Gregory, Research Historian, Tallahassee, Florida

Special Assistance
Bruce Graetz, Museum of Florida History, Tallahassee, Florida

Editor
Frederick P. Gaske, Historic Preservation Services, Tallahassee, Florida

Project Administration
Malinda Horton, Florida Association of Museums, Tallahassee, Florida

Graphic Design
Patti Cross, Osprey, Florida

This publication has been financed in part with historic preservation grant assistance provided by the
Division of Historical Resources, Florida Department of State, assisted by the Florida Historical Commission.
However, the contents and opinions do not necessarily reflect the views and opinions of the Florida Department of State,
nor does the mention of trade names or commercial products constitute endorsement or recommendation
by the Florida Department of State.

FLORIDA IN THE CIVIL WAR
1861-1865

Florida's role in the Civil War has not been as extensively examined as that of other Southern states, though in the past several decades it has received more scholarly attention. In many respects it remains the forgotten state of the Confederacy, just as it was during the 1860s, when a Northern newspaper referred to it as the "smallest tadpole in the dirty pool of secession."

Having ended its territorial period only in 1845 and still very much a frontier at the time of the Civil War, Florida nonetheless displayed characteristics of the other Deep South states of the Cotton Kingdom. A plantation belt, similar to that found in South Carolina,

Georgia, Alabama, and Mississippi, ran through the north-central portion of the peninsula from Marianna to Ocala. The 1860 census reported that Florida had a total population of only 140,424 with nearly 45 percent (61,745) of those being slaves. The largest settlements in Florida included Pensacola, Marianna, Apalachicola, Quincy, and Tallahassee in the west; Monticello, Madison, Lake City, Ocala, and Gainesville in the central portion of the state; Fernandina, Jacksonville, and St. Augustine along the east coast; and Key West in the south. With the exception of Key West, the southern half of the state was sparsely settled and consisted of a few small towns

concentrated around current or former military outposts. Some sugar production took place in the Manatee River area, and the southern region was also home to thousands of cattle that ranged the scrublands and swamps, awaiting shipment to Cuba or elsewhere.

By the early-to-mid 1800s, sectional disputes over slavery along with economic and political differences threatened national unity. These issues intensified in the decade following the Mexican War of 1846-1848 and culminated in 1860 with Republican Abraham Lincoln's election to the presidency. In the voting, Floridians supported Southern Democrat John C. Breckenridge over Constitutional Unionist candidate John Bell by a count of 8,543 to 5,437, while Lincoln did not even appear on the ballot in the South. In the gubernatorial race, Democrat John Milton defeated Constitutional Unionist Edward Hopkins by a comfortable margin. Milton, however, would not take office for one year; consequently Governor Madison Starke Perry would call for elections to a Secession Convention, to meet in Tallahassee in early 1861.

When the Secession Convention convened on January 3, 1861, a majority of the delegates seemed to support immediate secession, though a few opposed the concept completely and others supported it only in cooperation with other Southern states. Despite efforts of the latter groups, the convention voted 62-7 on January 10 to withdraw from the Union, making Florida the third state to do so after South Carolina and Mississippi. The following day they signed the Ordinance of Secession, temporarily making Florida an independent nation, though it would join the new Confederate States of America within a month. Throughout the state,

Secession Convention

Florida's Secession Convention began meeting in the state capitol on January 3, 1861. Delegates who opposed immediate secession, known as "cooperationists", introduced a proposal to have the convention's actions ratified in a statewide election, but it was not adopted. Instead the convention determined that it had the power to secede without ratification by popular vote. On January 9, the convention listened to a draft Ordinance of Secession, found it too ambiguous, and directed a committee to make revisions. The final version proclaimed Florida "a Sovereign and Independent Nation." Cooperationists made a series of last-ditch amendments, but they were defeated. The final vote on January 10 showed 62 delegates in support and seven opposed to secession.

On January 11, 1861, the delegates signed the document. An emotional moment occurred when cooperationist George T. Ward, who would die the following year at the Battle of Williamsburg, stated: "When I die I want it inscribed on my tombstone that I was the last man to give up the

Florida Ordinance of Secession, 1861.
(Image courtesy of the State Archives of Florida)

ship." James Owens countered with: "Unlike my friend Colonel Ward, I want it inscribed that I was the FIRST man to quit the rotten old hulk." With the document's signing, Florida became the third state to withdraw from the Union and soon became a member of the new Confederate States of America.

To learn more, see: "The Florida Secession Convention" by Ralph A. Wooster, *The Florida Historical Quarterly,* Vol. 36, No. 4, April 1958.

Confederate artillery battery at Pensacola, 1861. *(Image courtesy of the State Archives of Florida)*

secessionists celebrated the action, though Unionists like former territorial governor Richard Keith Call deplored the act. "You have opened the gates of Hell," he shouted to his detractors, "from which shall flow the curses of the damned which shall sink you to perdition."

At the time of the state's secession, Florida militia occupied Federal facilities around the state, taking control of the arsenal at Chattahoochee, Fort Clinch near Fernandina, and Fort Marion in St. Augustine. In Pensacola, Southern troops occupied Fort McRee, Fort Barrancas, and the Pensacola Navy Yard, leaving only Fort Pickens on Santa Rosa Island in Federal hands. At the southern end of the Florida peninsula, the Union retained Fort Jefferson in the Tortugas and Fort Taylor at Key West. These two locations later proved to be important points for the Union in enforcing the blockade of the Florida coast.

During the period from January through April 1861, tensions rose higher as the sectional crisis deepened with the secession of seven states and the formation of the Confederate States of America. For several months in early

1861, national attention was focused on Pensacola, as the possibility existed that hostilities might erupt there first. Instead the first fighting would occur in Charleston Harbor, with the April 1861 bombardment and surrender of Fort Sumter. Following its surrender, President Lincoln called for 75,000 troops to suppress the rebellion and four additional states joined the infant Confederacy.

Meanwhile, in Florida, Confederate troops strengthened their positions in an effort to force the Union troops out of Fort Pickens. No major fighting took place, however, until the night of October 8-9, when a Confederate force landed on Santa Rosa Island and attacked a Union camp. After a brisk engagement they soon withdrew, with casualties for the two sides numbering about 150. Subsequently, artillery bombardments occurred in November 1861 and in January 1862, but no further attempt was made by the Confederates to capture Fort Pickens.

In the spring of 1862, following reverses in the western theater of the war, Confederate troops withdrew from much of Florida, including Fernandina, St. Augustine, and Pensacola. In March 1862,

the Federals occupied Fernandina and St. Augustine and remained there for the duration of the war, and Jacksonville was occupied by the Federals for the first of four times during the war. Pensacola was abandoned by the Confederates in May 1862, and it stayed under Federal control for the remainder of the war.

The fourth occupation of Jacksonville, in February of 1864, led to the Battle of Olustee, the largest engagement of the war in Florida. It came about as the result of the Union desire to establish a loyal state government under the provisions of President Lincoln's 1863 Reconstruction Proclamation, as well as the desire to occupy the northeast portion of the state to recruit black troops and to disrupt Confederate supply activities. Union Brigadier General Truman Seymour, with a force of some 5,000 soldiers, including several regiments of black troops, moved west from Jacksonville in mid-February. Confederate Brigadier General Joseph Finegan, with reinforcements sent from Georgia, met the invading force with an approximately equal number of troops east of Olustee on February 20, 1864. The ensuing

Union occupation of Sanderson, Florida prior to the Battle of Olustee, 1864. *(Image courtesy of the State Archives of Florida)*

engagement was a clear Confederate victory, with Union soldiers retreating back to Jacksonville. One of the bloodiest battles of the war in terms of the percentage of casualties, Olustee stopped the Federal force from capturing Lake City. However in the aftermath, the Confederates were unable to dislodge the Federals from their positions around Jacksonville, which they retained for the remainder of the war.

In the fall of 1864, military activity increased in west Florida, culminating in the Battle of Marianna on September 27. During this engagement, a Union cavalry force under the command of Brigadier General Alexander Asboth, which included black troops and Florida Unionists, had a bloody encounter with a ragtag collection of assorted Confederate defenders, including old men and young boys. The Union forces occupied and burned part of the town before withdrawing.

A final Confederate victory occurred in Florida in March 1865, shortly before the end of the war, at the Battle of Natural Bridge. It began with a Federal landing near the St. Marks Lighthouse on the Gulf coast south of Tallahassee in a move intended to eliminate that area from being used by blockade runners, while a Union naval force also ascended the St. Marks River to attack a Confederate fort located there. After occupying the port of St. Marks, the Federals might then be in a position to move against the capital. Confederate troops defended a bridge over the St. Marks River at Newport, forcing Brigadier General John Newton's Federals to march northward and attempt to cross at Natural Bridge. A hastily assembled Confederate force

★ ★

1860

October 1	Democrat John Milton is elected governor of Florida.
November 6	Republican Abraham Lincoln is elected president of the United States.
November 26	Florida Governor Madison Starke Perry asks state legislature to call for a secession convention.
December 20	South Carolina becomes the first state to secede from the Union.

1861

January 3	Florida Secession Convention convenes in Tallahassee.
January 6-7	State troops occupy Chattahoochee Arsenal, Fort Marion in St. Augustine, and Fort Clinch on Amelia Island. Fort Taylor in Key West and Fort Jefferson in the Tortugas remain in Federal hands.
January 10	Florida Secession Convention votes 62-7 to secede from the Union. Ordinance of Secession is signed the next day.

	Union troops in Pensacola abandon Forts Barrancas and McRee and move to the more defensible Fort Pickens on Santa Rosa Island.
January 12	Alabama and Florida troops receive the surrender of the Pensacola Navy Yard, and unsuccessfully demand the surrender of Fort Pickens.
February 4	Delegates from the seceded states, including Florida, meet in Montgomery, Alabama to organize the Confederate States of America.
February 9	Jefferson Davis is elected provisional president of the Confederate States of America.
February 25	Jefferson Davis nominates Stephen R. Mallory of Key West as Confederate Secretary of the Navy.
March 4	Abraham Lincoln is inaugurated president of the United States.
April 12	Confederate forces fire on Fort Sumter in Charleston Harbor, South Carolina, forcing its surrender the next day. Union forces land on Santa Rosa Island to reinforce the garrison at

Union Gunboat *Mohawk* at St. Marks Lighthouse, 1862. *(Image courtesy of the State Archives of Florida)*

of some 1,000 men under the command of Brigadier General William Miller, including cadets from the West Florida Seminary (present-day Florida State University) in Tallahassee, defended the crossing. More than 600 Union black soldiers attacked the Confederate positions at Natural Bridge on March 6, but were repulsed. Following their defeat, the Federal land force returned to the coast. The Union ships were also unsuccessful in their efforts to reach the Confederate fort at St. Marks. The Confederate victory at Natural Bridge

helped ensure that Tallahassee would remain the only Confederate capital east of the Mississippi River to not be captured before the war's close.

The Confederacy's collapse came in the spring of 1865. By that time, Confederate control of Florida was limited to the interior north and central portions of the state. On April 1, Governor John Milton committed suicide at his home near Marianna. Eight days later, General Robert E. Lee's Army of Northern Virginia surrendered at Appomattox in Virginia. Other Florida

units capitulated with General Joseph E. Johnston's army in North Carolina on April 26. In May and early June, the remaining Confederate troops in Florida laid down their weapons.

The Civil War impacted not only Floridians who served in the military, but those who labored on the home front as well. Included in this category were males too young or old for military service, white females, and the state's African American population. When the war began, some of the strongest Florida pro-Confederate "fire-eaters"

★★

	Fort Pickens. Three days later, President Lincoln calls for 75,000 troops to put down the rebellion in the seceded states.
April 19	President Lincoln proclaims a blockade of the seceded states, including Florida.
July 21	First major battle of the war is fought near Bull Run (Manassas), Virginia. No Florida military units participate, though Floridian Brigadier General Edmund Kirby Smith is prominently involved and is wounded in the battle.
October 7	John Milton is inaugurated Florida governor.
October 9	A Confederate force, including two companies of Floridians, lands on Santa Rosa Island, east of Fort Pickens, and attacks the camp of the 6th New York Infantry Regiment. Reinforcements from the fort force the Confederates to withdraw.
November 22-23	Federal forces at Fort Pickens engage in a massive artillery duel with Confederate batteries around Pensacola. An estimated 5,000 cannon balls and shells are fired during the bombardment, which damages Pensacola Navy Yard, Fort McRee and the towns of Warrington and Pensacola.

1862

January 1-2	A second artillery bombardment takes place between Union and Confederate batteries at Pensacola. There are few casualties, but some damage is inflicted on Pensacola Navy Yard.
January 16	Union naval forces attack Cedar Key, the western terminus of the Florida Railroad.
March 2-4	Confederate forces evacuate Amelia Island, including Fort Clinch, which is then occupied by Union troops.
March 10-11	St. Augustine is evacuated by Confederate forces and occupied by the Federals.
March 12	Jacksonville is occupied by Federal forces. It will be evacuated the following month.
April 6-7	Battle of Shiloh, Tennessee takes place. A Florida battalion participates and suffers heavy losses.
May 9-12	Pensacola is abandoned by Confederate forces and occupied by the Union.

Union soldiers in camp at Jacksonville. *(Image courtesy of the State Archives of Florida)*

were women. They produced uniforms and equipment for soldiers, as well as unit flags under which their men would fight. Sewing societies continued to provide such necessities throughout the conflict. Their efforts became even more important as the war progressed and the Confederate supply system deteriorated. Governor Milton expressed his gratitude to Florida

women for their "generous, patriotic, and untiring efforts to clothe our gallant soldiers." In addition, women contributed to the war effort by serving as nurses or matrons in hospitals, in raising money for relief activities, and in maintaining morale among those in the military and at home. They also managed farms and plantations in the absence of enlisted husbands, fathers, and sons.

Floridians on the home front suffered from the constant threat of Union occupation. Citizens in Key West remained under the control of Federal forces throughout the war, while those in Apalachicola, Cedar Key, Fernandina, Jacksonville, Palatka, Pensacola, St. Augustine, Tampa, and other towns faced either long-term or occasional occupations. Florida civilians faced growing shortages of luxury items and many necessities as well. Salt became unobtainable from pre-war sources, and Floridians turned to the state's long coastline for the boiling of seawater to produce the vital commodity used in the preservation of meat. Coffee, white sugar, and many other foodstuffs were not available, or could be found only at exorbitant prices. The same was true with clothing, particularly shoes. Various substitutes were resorted to, including drinking coffee made with cottonseed

★ ★

May 31 Florida troops participate in the Battle of Seven Pines, Virginia where they capture a Federal artillery battery but suffer heavy casualties.

September 17 Florida troops are engaged at the Battle of Antietam (Sharpsburg), Maryland, the bloodiest single-day battle of the war. Five days later, President Lincoln issues preliminary Emancipation Proclamation.

September 30-October 13 Federal naval and land forces mount an expedition to St. Johns Bluff. The position is abandoned by its Confederate defenders on October 2, and Jacksonville is temporarily occupied for a second time.

1863

January 1 Final Emancipation Proclamation issued.

March 10 Jacksonville is occupied for a third time by Union forces. It will be evacuated once again at the end of the month. The occupation forces include Union black soldiers, making it one of the earliest operations involving their use. Several skirmishes will occur in the vicinity during the occupation.

July 1-3 Battle of Gettysburg, Pennsylvania takes place. A brigade of Floridians, consisting of the 2nd, 5th, and 8th Florida Infantry Regiments, participates and suffers heavy casualties.

September 19-20 Battle of Chickamauga, Georgia, one of the bloodiest battles of the war, takes place. Seven Florida units participate and suffer heavy losses.

1864

February 7 Union forces occupy Jacksonville for the fourth time during the war. This final occupation will last until the war's end.

February 20 Battle of Olustee, the largest and bloodiest battle in the state during the conflict, takes place. Union forces are defeated and retreat back to their Jacksonville defenses.

April 1 The Union transport ship *Maple Leaf* is sunk in the St. Johns River by a Confederate mine.

May 6 Union forces temporarily occupy Tampa and Fort Brooke.

May 19 Union forces from Fort Myers raid Fort Meade.

May 23 Confederate forces under Captain J.J. Dickison capture the USS *Columbine* on the St. Johns River.

and making hats and shoes from palmetto leaves and corn shucks.

The war most profoundly affected Florida's African American population, which included 61,745 slaves and a small number of free blacks. Some slaves remained with their owners throughout the war, while others fled to Union-occupied sections of the state. Many enlisted in the Union army and navy. In addition to forced labor on farms and plantations, the enslaved population was frequently impressed by the Confederate government for military-related tasks, such as building fortifications. Concerned over possible revolts, white Floridians maintained slave patrols during the war. To ensure slave productivity and maintain the safety of the white population, a provision of the first Confederate Conscription Act exempted one white male from military service for every twenty slaves. The end of the war and the subsequent passage of the Thirteenth Amendment brought freedom to black Floridians, though true social, political, and economic equality proved much more elusive.

The Union blockade of the Florida coast also had an important impact on the state. Upon the war's outbreak, the U.S. Navy implemented a blockade along the southern coast, with the South Atlantic and the East Gulf Blockading Squadrons having jurisdiction over Florida's extensive coastline. While the state had few major ports within its borders, its numerous coves and bays and its proximity to both Cuba and the Bahamas made it a popular location for blockade running, particularly in small,

Slaves escaping to a Union blockading vessel off St. Marks, 1862.
(Image courtesy of the State Archives of Florida)

shallow-draft vessels. The blockade initially proved porous, but it became more successful as the war progressed, with the East Gulf Blockading Squadron alone capturing or destroying 283 vessels. While blockade runners brought in much needed medicine, weapons, and equipment, they also wasted precious cargo space on profitable luxury items and contributed to the continued production of cotton, which commanded a high price in Europe, rather than the growing of vital food crops.

★ ★

August 17   Union forces are routed by Confederate troops led by Captain J.J. Dickison at the Battle of Gainesville.

September 27   Battle of Marianna takes place. Union troops, including elements of the 1st Florida Union Cavalry, rout the Confederate defenders and briefly occupy the town.

1865

February 13   Confederate troops led by Captain J.J. Dickison fight a daylong skirmish with a Union raiding force at Station Number 4 near Cedar Key.

February 20   A Confederate force mounts an unsuccessful attack on Union-held Fort Myers.

March 4   Abraham Lincoln inaugurated for a second term as president.

March 4-5   Union expedition lands near the St. Marks Lighthouse.

March 6   Battle of Natural Bridge takes place. Union troops are stopped in their attempt to cross the St. Marks River and retreat back to ships waiting along the coast. Tallahassee remains the only Confederate state capital east of the Mississippi River to not be captured until the end of the war.

April 1   Governor John Milton commits suicide at his home near Marianna. Abraham Allison becomes acting governor.

April 9   The Army of Northern Virginia, including the remnants of the Florida Brigade, is surrendered at Appomattox Court House, Virginia.

April 14   President Abraham Lincoln is shot and mortally wounded at Ford's Theater in Washington, D.C. He dies the following morning.

April 26   The Army of Tennessee, including the Florida Brigade, is surrendered in North Carolina. The surrender also includes all Confederate forces in Florida.

May 10   Union Brigadier General Edward McCook enters Tallahassee to accept the surrender of Confederate forces. A formal transfer of power ceremony and announcement of the Emancipation Proclamation takes place ten days later.

July 13   William Marvin is appointed provisional governor of Florida.

1866

April 2   President Andrew Johnson officially proclaims the insurrection in Florida and nine other ex-Confederate states to be at an end.

Confederate cavalry crossing the St. Johns River, from *Dickison and His Men.*
(Image courtesy of the State Archives of Florida)

Florida's contributions to the Confederate economy were significant. Beef from the central and southern portions of the state became an increasingly important source of supply to Confederate armies, especially during the later stages of the war. Federal forces made efforts to stop the flow of beef northward, while a Confederate "Cow Cavalry" was established to protect the herds from Union threats. This led to a small-scale, yet vicious "cattle war" in southern Florida during 1864-1865. Florida's salt production was essential for curing the beef and pork used by both the military and civilian populations. As the war continued, many Florida saltworks became the target of Union naval attacks.

Anti-war sentiment increased during the course of the war. Conscription, adopted in 1862, proved unpopular and led some Floridians to "lay-out" in remote areas of the state to avoid military service. The impressment of goods by the Confederate government and the adoption of an unpopular tax-in-kind, coupled with inflation and wartime shortages, led to a surge in anti-war or pro-Union sentiment. Consequently, as historian John E. Johns writes, "[b]y the spring of 1865 the desire for an end to hostilities was general throughout the state."

Nevertheless, more than 15,000 Floridians served in the Confederate military, most outside the borders of the state. Florida regiments took part in virtually all of the major battles of the Civil War, in both the eastern and western theaters, where separate Florida Brigades fought valiantly and suffered heavy casualties. Reflecting the fraternal nature of the conflict, white Florida Unionists manned two cavalry regiments and a small artillery battery, and more than 1,000 African Americans from Florida joined the Union army as well. Additionally, numbers of white Unionists and escaped black slaves served in the Federal naval squadrons that blockaded the state. High ranking Confederate officers from Florida included generals James Patton Anderson, Theodore Brevard, William Davis, Joseph Finegan,

William Loring, William Miller, Edward Perry, and Edmund Kirby Smith, while Stephen Mallory was Secretary of the Navy. Additionally, several Florida-born officers rose to the rank of general in the Union army.

The Civil War represented a watershed event and major turning point in American history. It ended slavery and the concept of secession, and cemented the dominance of national rights and the national government over states' rights. Floridians, both white and black, and male and female, were deeply affected by the war. Unionist white Floridians celebrated victory, while the pro-Confederate majority accepted defeat; both groups strove to rebuild their lives after the conflict's end. African Americans in Florida endured the war years, rejoiced over emancipation, and faced the Reconstruction years with cautious optimism. Though it would take decades, Florida, the least populous and perhaps least significant Confederate state, eventually emerged from the war's aftermath as a major power in the New South.

Dr. David J. Coles, Chair
Department of History, Political
Science and Philosophy
Longwood University
Farmville, Virginia

Union soldiers at Fort Marion, St. Augustine, 1865. *(Image courtesy of the State Archives of Florida)*

—— Bay County ——

Lynn Haven

UNION SOLDIER MONUMENT
Memorial Park
Eighth Street and Georgia Avenue

Founded by New York developer W. H. Lynn, the community was developed as a home for Union veterans of the Civil War. Articles in the Union veterans' Grand Army of the Republic (GAR) newspaper, *The National Tribune,* generated interest in this chance to live in Florida. The first land offerings occurred in January 1911 and the first building was erected the following March. The Ladies Auxiliary of the GAR received land from Lynn's company for a GAR hall and a cemetery. Dedicated in September 1911, the Lynn Haven Cemetery contains the remains of over 100 Union veterans. In 1913, Union veterans began planning a memorial to their fellow soldiers. Underwritten by donations from GAR members, this statue of a Union soldier was constructed in 1920 and dedicated on February 12, 1921, the anniversary of Abraham Lincoln's birthday. Resting on a 40-foot high pedestal, this statue faces north and is reported to be one of the first privately funded Union monuments in the South not located in a cemetery.

Union Soldier Monument, Lynn Haven.
(Image courtesy of William Lees, Florida Public Archaeology Network)

Salt kettle, Oaks By The Bay Park, Panama City.
(Image courtesy of William Lees, Florida Public Archaeology Network)

Panama City

CONFEDERATE SALT KETTLE
Oaks By The Bay Park
Chestnut Avenue and West 9th Street

A major contribution of Florida to the Confederate war effort was the production of salt. Salt was necessary for preserving meat and other perishable foods but could not be imported due to the Union blockade. Produced by boiling sea water in iron kettles, massive saltworks were established along St. Andrew Bay during the war. This site includes a salt kettle placed here by the United Daughters of the Confederacy in 1960, a dedication plaque, and an interpretive plaque explaining the history of salt-making during the Civil War. A second salt kettle is on display at the James R. Asbell Park.

ST. ANDREW BAY SALTWORKS STATE HISTORICAL MARKER
James R. Asbell Park
West Beach Drive and Caroline Boulevard

The text of this State Historical Marker reads: Between 1861 and 1865, the St. Andrew Bay Saltworks, one of the largest producers of salt in the South, contributed to the Confederate cause by providing salt, fish and cattle for southern troops and citizens. A necessary preservative in those times, salt sold for as much as $50 per bushel, and was produced in wood-fired saltworks on the perimeter of the West Bay, East Bay and North Bay and Lake Powell (a.k.a. Lake Ocala). An estimated 2,500 men, primarily from Florida, Georgia and Alabama, were exempted from combat duty in order to labor in the saltworks. The salt was transported to Eufaula, Alabama, then to Montgomery, for distribution throughout the Confederate states. Because of the importance of St. Andrew Bay Saltworks to the Confederacy, Acting Master W. R. Browne, commander of the USS *Restless,* was instructed to commence a series of assaults beginning in August 1862. In December 1863, additional Union attacks occurred, which Confederate home guards could not resist. The attacks resulted in the destruction of more than 290 saltworks, valued by Master Browne at more than $3,000,000. The St. Andrew Bay Saltworks employees promptly rebuilt them, and they remained in operation through February 1865.

ST. ANDREW SKIRMISH STATE HISTORICAL MARKER
West Beach Drive and Friendship Avenue

The text of this State Historical Marker reads: Near this site on March 20, 1863, Confederate soldiers commanded by Captain Walter J. Robinson repelled a landing by Union sailors led by Acting Master James Folger of the blockading vessel USS *Roebuck.* The 11-man scouting party of Union sailors was seeking to locate a southern civilian vessel near the "Old Town" spring, when they were reportedly ordered to surrender by Captain Robinson. During the ensuing skirmish, several Union sailors were killed and wounded as they fled to their launch boat. Quarter, or safe passage, was requested by the remaining Union sailors to retrieve their dead and wounded. Total Union casualties were six dead and three wounded. Union sailors buried four of the deceased on nearby Hurricane Island, and a fifth sailor was interred by the Confederate soldiers. No casualties were recorded by the Confederate unit, which later became Company A of the 11th Florida Infantry Regiment. After the conclusion of the Civil War, the remains of the Union sailors were removed to the national cemetery at Fort Barrancas.

—— Escambia County ——

Pensacola

By the time of the Civil War, Pensacola was an important Gulf Coast shipping port and railroad transportation center. It was the southern terminus of the Alabama & Florida Railroad which ran to Montgomery, Alabama, while the Pensacola & Mobile Railroad ran from the Perdido River to a junction with the Alabama & Florida Railroad

about 14 miles north of the city. It was also a center for commercial lumbering mills and an important military center with a large Navy Yard and three forts, Fort Pickens, Fort McRee and Fort Barrancas, protecting the entrance to the harbor. The defenses at Fort Barrancas included the Advanced Redoubt and the Battery San Antonio or Water Battery. Under pressure from Southern militia after Florida's secession in January 1861, Union forces at Fort Barrancas and Pensacola Navy Yard withdrew to the

more defensible Fort Pickens. They also abandoned Fort McRee after disabling its guns and dumping its gunpowder into the water. After the Union commander, Lieutenant Adam Slemmer, refused Southern demands to surrender Fort Pickens, an agreement was reached between Southern senators and President James Buchanan's administration. Under this unofficial "armistice", Slemmer's garrison would not be reinforced and the Southern forces would not attack Fort Pickens. This changed, however, with the firing on Fort Sumter in Charleston Harbor on April 12, 1861. In September 1861, Union troops from Fort Pickens conducted two raids directed at the Navy Yard. The Confederates retaliated by conducting a night attack against the Union encampment east of Fort Pickens in October 1861. In the ensuing Battle of Santa Rosa Island, the Confederate force destroyed the camp of the 6th New York Volunteers and then withdrew to their boats while fighting off a counterattack from Union troops sent out from Fort Pickens. (See the "Battle of Santa Rosa Island" sidebar for more information.) On November 22-23, 1861, Union forces at Fort Pickens and on their warships, the USS *Niagara* and the USS *Richmond*, engaged the Confederates in massive artillery duels. The Navy Yard and Fort McRee were extensively damaged but casualties were minimal on both sides. A second artillery duel on January 1-2, 1862 caused further damage to the Navy Yard but few casualties. The stalemate continued until May 1862, when Confederate troops razed the Navy Yard and withdrew from Pensacola to reinforce their hard-pressed forces in Tennessee. Pensacola and the surrounding military facilities were quickly occupied by Union forces. Pensacola Bay remained securely in Union control throughout the remainder of the war, serving as a center of operations for the Union navy's West Gulf Blockading Squadron and as a base for Union army operations into West Florida and Alabama.

Union raid on a Florida Confederate saltworks, 1862. *(Image courtesy of the State Archives of Florida)*

Salt

A vital commodity used in the preservation of meat and fish, salt was one of the most important resources produced in Florida for the Confederacy. The war's outbreak brought a blockade of Southern ports by the Union navy and the cutting off of the supply of salt from the North. Within a short period of time the price of the commodity had risen to an exorbitant level, and Southerners looked for new sources.

Florida's long coastline provided part of the answer, as seawater could be boiled to produce the necessary article. The largest operations were established on the central and northern Gulf Coast and, by 1863, the main Florida saltworks produced more than 7,500 bushels per day. However,

the saltworks, with their vulnerable locations along the coastline, became the targets of raids by the Union navy. Federal officials complained that the saltmaking operations sprang up again almost as soon as the raiders had left. Nevertheless, the Union attacks were so worrisome that Florida Governor John Milton made efforts to station Confederate troops along the coast, and also authorized the saltmakers to organize themselves into military companies for defense. Despite the Union raids, the production of the vital commodity continued until the end of the war.

To learn more, see: "The Extent and Importance of Federal Naval Raids on Salt-Making in Florida, 1862-1865" by Ella Lonn, *The Florida Historical Quarterly*, Vol. 10, No. 4, April 1932.

Fort Barrancas, Pensacola. *(Image courtesy of William Lees, Florida Public Archaeology Network)*

BARRANCAS NATIONAL CEMETERY
Pensacola Naval Air Station
80 Hovey Road
850.453.4108
www.cem.va.gov/cems/nchp/barrancas.asp

In 1868, the U.S. Navy Yard Cemetery at the Marine Hospital was transferred to the War Department and designated the Barrancas National Cemetery. Sections 1 thru 12 of the cemetery contain the remains of 1,239 Union Civil War casualties, as well as the remains of 72 Confederate soldiers. The Union dead include troops stationed at Pensacola and bodies removed from Bayou Chico, Gunboat Point and Santa Rosa Island in Escambia County, East Pass in Okaloosa County, Apalachicola in Franklin County, St. Andrew Bay in Bay County, and Marianna in Jackson County. Among the Union dead are 650 white Union soldiers, 252 U.S. Colored Troops, and 337 officers and sailors of the Union navy. Other sections of the cemetery also contain the remains of

Florida Civil War casualties relocated there after the war. An example of this occurred in 1927 when the U.S. military abandoned the Key West Post Cemetery, and its 468 burials, many of them Union yellow fever casualties, were disinterred and reburied at the Barrancas National Cemetery.

FORT BARRANCAS
Taylor Road
850.934.2600
www.nps.gov/guis/planyourvisit/fort-barrancas.htm

One of three forts designed to protect the United States Navy Yard, Fort Barrancas was completed in 1844 on a bluff overlooking Pensacola Bay. Defenses included two other major separate masonry fortifications. The Advanced Redoubt Battery was constructed beginning in 1845, approximately one half mile inland, to protect the fort from attack on the land side. The 1797 Spanish Battery San Antonio, or Water Battery, immediately south of the fort on the shore side, was renovated in 1840. With the

election of Abraham Lincoln as President in 1860, and the secession of Florida in January of the following year, the Union garrison abandoned Fort Barrancas in favor of the more defensible Fort Pickens on Santa Rosa Island. Southern forces occupied this site at that point and Fort Barrancas took part in the massive artillery duels with Fort Pickens in November 1861 and January 1862. After the Confederates abandoned Pensacola in May 1862, Fort Barrancas became an important base for Union operations into Florida and Alabama for the duration of the war. Like other masonry fortifications, Fort Barrancas became obsolete with the advances in artillery and naval armaments after the Civil War. Today, Fort Barrancas is a unit of the National Park Service's Gulf Islands National Seashore. A visitor center exhibit provides a history of the fort during the Civil War. Two Civil War era buildings from the Fort Barrancas Cantonment, the fort hospital and an officers quarters, are now located on the grounds of the Pensacola Naval Air Station.

Fort Pickens, Pensacola. *(Image courtesy of William Lees, Florida Public Archaeology Network)*

FORT PICKENS
Santa Rosa Island
850.934.2600
www.nps.gov/guis/planyourvisit/fort-pickens.htm

Completed in 1834 on the western tip of Santa Rosa Island in Pensacola Bay, Fort Pickens is the largest of the three forts constructed to defend the Pensacola Navy Yard. When Florida seceded from the Union in January 1861, the Navy Yard and all of the defensive fortifications on the mainland side of Pensacola Bay were occupied by Florida and Alabama troops, but Fort Pickens on Santa Rosa Island remained in Union hands. Union troops from Fort Pickens conducted two raids directed at the Navy Yard in September 1861. In October 1861, at the Battle of Santa Rosa Island, a Confederate force of 1,200 men staged a night-time raid against the Union encampment east of Fort Pickens. In November 1861 and January 1862, Union forces at Fort Pickens and on U.S. Navy vessels engaged the Confederates at Fort McRee and Fort Barrancas in massive artillery duels. Responding to a need for troops in Tennessee, the Confederates abandoned Pensacola to Union forces in May 1862.

Fort Pickens remained in Union control for the duration of the war, serving as a base for military operations. Fort Pickens and the Santa Rosa Island battlefield are located in the National Park Service's Gulf Islands National Seashore. Guided and self-guided tours are available at the visitor center, and interpretive signage is located throughout the fort. A State Historical Marker for "Captain Richard Bradford" is located at the Santa Rosa Island battlefield in the vicinity of where Captain Bradford became the first Confederate officer from Florida to be killed in the war.

Battle of Santa Rosa Island, 1861. *(Image courtesy of the State Archives of Florida)*

Battle of Santa Rosa Island

Following Florida's secession in January 1861, state troops occupied the Pensacola Navy Yard, Fort Barrancas, and Fort McRee, while Fort Pickens, located on Santa Rosa Island, remained in Union hands. During the spring and summer of 1861, Confederate troops strengthened the fortifications facing Fort Pickens, while Federal officials reinforced the fort's garrison. Though expected, no major fighting took place during the summer.

In early October, however, the Confederates began planning a raid against Santa Rosa Island. The force selected for the operation consisted of 1,200 men under the command of Brigadier General Richard H. Anderson. On the night of October 8, they were loaded aboard barges and towed across the bay, landing after midnight on October 9 four miles to the east of Fort Pickens. They had advanced about three miles towards the fort before encountering the camp of the 6th New York Infantry. The Federals put up a brief resistance before fleeing. Anderson contemplated an attack on the fort itself, but with daylight approaching and surprise lost, he ordered a return to their boats. Federals from the fort skirmished with the retreating Confederates. The Union forces lost 67 killed, wounded, missing or captured, while the Confederates suffered 87 casualties.

To learn more, see: "Battle of Santa Rosa Island" by J.L. Larkin, *The Florida Historical Quarterly,* Vol. 37, Nos. 3 & 4, January & April 1959.

HISTORIC PENSACOLA VILLAGE
850.595.5985

www.historicpensacola.org

Historic Pensacola Village consists of 27 historic properties, including:

Old Christ Church
405 South Adams Street

Constructed in 1832, this church building was used by Union troops during the Federal occupation of Pensacola as a hospital, barracks, and military chapel.

T.T. Wentworth Jr. Florida State Museum
330 South Jefferson Street

Located in the restored 1908 Old City Hall building, the Wentworth Museum contains exhibits on local history including "The Coming of Civil War" exhibit on the first floor and a larger "Pensacolians and the Civil War" exhibit on the second floor with period artifacts and historic photographs. Many of the Florida Civil War items on display were obtained from the Civil War Soldiers Museum in Pensacola which closed after it was damaged by Hurricane Ivan in 2004.

Pensacola Historical Museum
115 East Zaragoza Street

Located across the street from the Wentworth Museum in the restored 1881 Arbona Building, the museum contains additional exhibits on local history including "Pensacola in the Civil War" in the "A Military Town" gallery with period artifacts and historic photographs.

Hyer-Knowles Mill, Pensacola.
(Image courtesy of William Lees, Florida Public Archaeology Network)

HYER-KNOWLES PLANING MILL
Chimney Park
Scenic Highway and Langley Avenue

www.pensapedia.com/wiki/Chimney_Park

Constructed in c.1854 on land owned by lumber manufacturer and merchant Henry Hyer, the Hyer-Knowles Planing Mill was one of the many lumber mills built in the Pensacola area prior to the Civil War. In addition to planed lumber, the mill produced shingles and lathe products. During the Confederate evacuation of Pensacola in March 1862, the mill was stripped of its machinery and its buildings burned to prevent it from falling into Union hands. The remnants of a massive thirty-foot brick chimney made of locally manufactured brick, which was part of the mill's steam power plant, are located on the property. In the 1980s, the property was purchased by the City of Pensacola for use as a park. A State Historical Marker at the park provides information on the mill's history.

LEE SQUARE
North Palafox Street

www.pensapedia.com/wiki/Lee_Square

At this site in 1862, Union forces constructed Fort McClellan, an earthenworks fortification, which was one of a series of defenses along the perimeter of Pensacola. In 1889, the Florida Square Park was renamed for Confederate General Robert E. Lee. A Confederate monument was erected in the park by the local Ladies Monument Association in 1891.

Confederate Monument, Lee Square, Pensacola.
(Image courtesy of William Lees, Florida Public Archaeology Network)

Wentworth Museum, Pensacola. *(Image courtesy of William Lees, Florida Public Archaeology Network)*

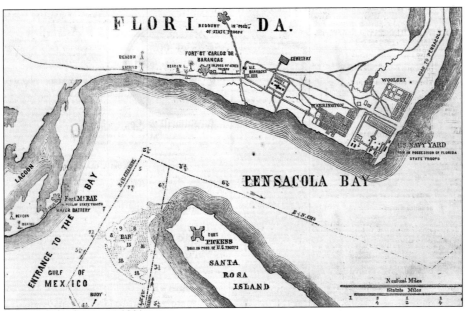

Pensacola Harbor map, 1861. *(Image courtesy of the State Archives of Florida)*

PENSACOLA LIGHTHOUSE
Pensacola Naval Air Station
850.637.4050
www.pensacolalighthouse.org

In the spring of 1861, Confederate authorities dismantled and removed the first-order Fresnel lens from the 1859 Pensacola Lighthouse. During the Union bombardment of Pensacola in November 1861, the lighthouse was struck by several shells and slightly damaged. After Union troops reoccupied the city in 1862, the lighthouse was relit with a smaller fourth-order Fresnel lens in December of that year. The Pensacola Lighthouse Association provides lighthouse tours and operates the Richard C. Callaway Museum in the restored 1869 Lighthouse Keeper's Quarters.

PENSACOLA NAVY YARD
Pensacola Naval Air Station
190 Radford Boulevard
850.452.0111

Two Civil War era buildings from the Pensacola Navy Yard, a storehouse and the combination chapel/armory building, remain on what is now part of Pensacola Naval Air Station. The Navy Yard's brick boundary wall, gatehouses, bulkhead, and wet basin from the Civil War period also survive. The bulkhead and wet basin originally formed part of the Yard's ship construction and repair facility. Construction on the Navy Yard

began in 1826. In the years leading up to the Civil War, it became a major facility for U.S. Navy shipbuilding, repair, and supply. In January 1861, Southern troops from Florida and Alabama occupied the Navy Yard. In September 1861, Union forces from Fort Pickens launched two raids directed against the Confederate-held Navy Yard. On September 2, the first Union raid destroyed a huge scuttled drydock which the Confederates had planned to refloat and sink in the channel. The raid was accomplished without casualties on either side. The second Union raid, on September 14, resulted in the burning of the armed Confederate schooner *Judah* and the spiking of a Confederate Columbiad gun at the nearby battery. During this raid, Union forces suffered three dead and thirteen wounded, while Confederate forces suffered three dead and an undetermined number of wounded. In November 1861 and January 1862, the Navy Yard suffered extensive damage when Union forces at Fort Pickens and on U.S. Navy vessels engaged the Confederates in massive artillery duels. In May 1862, Confederate forces withdrew from Pensacola, in the process stripping the Navy Yard of its valuable machinery and setting fire to the facility. Union forces reoccupied the Navy Yard and immediately began to clear away the rubble and erect new structures. Shortly thereafter, Union Rear Admiral

David G. Farragut inspected the Yard and concluded that it could be repaired adequately to serve as a naval depot for his West Gulf Blockading Squadron. The Squadron used the Pensacola Navy Yard as an operational base for the remainder of the Civil War.

ST. JOHNS CEMETERY
301 North G Street
www.stjohnshistoriccemetery.org

In this cemetery are the graves of 89 Confederate dead, including Augustus E. Maxwell, who was elected Senator to the Confederate Congress in 1862 and served until 1865; Brigadier General Edward A. Perry, who commanded the Florida Brigade in the Army of Northern Virginia and was Governor of Florida from 1885 to 1889; Major General Samuel G. French, a divisional commander in the Army of Tennessee; and Brigadier General William Miller, the Confederate field commander at the Battle of Natural Bridge.

Mallory Gravesite, St. Michael's Cemetery, Pensacola.
(Image courtesy of William Lees, Florida Public Archaeology Network)

ST. MICHAEL'S CEMETERY
6 North Alcaniz Street
850.436.4643
www.stmichaelscemetery.org

This cemetery contains the remains of 100 Confederate dead including Stephen R. Mallory, Confederate Secretary of the Navy, and Delity P. Kelly, a Confederate army nurse who is believed to be the only Florida female to receive a state Civil War veteran's pension for military service.

— Franklin County —

Apalachicola

By the time of the Civil War, Apalachicola was Florida's largest cotton port and the third largest cotton port on the entire Gulf of Mexico coast behind only New Orleans and Mobile. An active area for blockade running, Union naval vessels of the Gulf Coast Blockading Squadron began closing off the city in June 1861, and most seaborne commerce was effectively halted during the war. Throughout the war, the Apalachicola vicinity was also an active area for Confederate salt production. As Confederate forces in the area were sent to other locations in early 1862 and the city was left almost defenseless, most of the population fled inland, many of them to Ricco's Bluff some 90 miles up the Apalachicola River. In April 1862, a small detachment of Union sailors and marines from the USS *Sagamore* and the USS *Mercedita* landed at Apalachicola, but withdrew back to their ships after one night. Although never occupied permanently, Union forces periodically returned to the mostly abandoned city during the remainder of the war.

CHESTNUT STREET CEMETERY
Avenue E between 6th and 8th Streets

This cemetery contains the remains of at least 76 Confederate soldiers and sailors, including local veterans such as the three Raney brothers and William Orman, as well as veterans of Confederate units from other states such as Georgia, Texas, and Virginia. A State Historical Marker at the cemetery states that seven of the Confederate soldiers buried here participated in the Battle of Gettysburg as members of the Florida Brigade. The cemetery also contains the remains of Union veterans.

ORMAN HOUSE HISTORIC STATE PARK
177 5th Street
850.653.1209
www.floridastateparks.org/ormanhouse

Using lumber pre-measured and cut at Syracuse, New York and shipped to

Orman House, Apalachicola.
(Image courtesy of the Florida Park Service)

Florida, businessman Thomas Orman built this house overlooking Scipio Creek and the Apalachicola River in 1838. House features incorporate details of both Federal and Greek Revival styles. Having arrived from a plantation north of Marianna, Orman quickly gained prominence in Apalachicola as a highly successful mercantile store proprietor, shipping owner, and cotton merchant. As a Confederate sympathizer, Orman was arrested and detained for a short time by Union authorities during the Civil War. His 26 slaves were freed by Union troops and transported to Union-held Key West. Local lore tells of Mrs. Sarah Orman sending warning signals from the captain's walk platform on the roof of the house to Confederate soldiers up river when Union troops were in the city. It is also reported that a brick outbuilding on the property served as a hospital during the war. The Ormans' only child, William Thomas, served in the 1st Florida Infantry as a lieutenant, and after the war as a state legislator and senator. Ironically, Thomas Orman was also arrested and detained by Confederate authorities on suspicion of Union sympathies at one point during the war when he traveled to Marianna, but was released after Governor John Milton intervened on his behalf.

RANEY HOUSE
128 Market Street
850.653.1700
www.apalachicolahistoricalsociety.org

David Raney, a newly arrived merchant from Virginia, constructed a Federal-style house on this site in 1838, and added Greek Revival features to it around 1850. During the Civil War, three of Raney's sons, David, Jr., Edward, and George, served in the Confederate forces. David Raney, Jr. served in the 1st Florida Infantry and then as a lieutenant in the Confederate Marine Corps. He was in command of the Marine detachment on the ironclad CSS *Tennessee* when it was forced to surrender at the Battle of Mobile Bay in August 1864. Captured and imprisoned at New Orleans, he escaped in October 1864 and returned to duty. Edward Raney served in the 2nd Florida Cavalry and George Raney served in the Confederate infantry. The Raney parents and their three young daughters left Apalachicola when the city was threatened by the Union navy and fled to Bainbridge, Georgia. Legend relates that the ladies of Apalachicola met in the Raney House early in the war to sew a unit flag for local troops. Another legend relates that Franklin County troops were mustered out of service at this site at the end of the war. Exhibits include period furnishings, documents and artifacts, including a collection of Confederate bonds and currency.

TRINITY EPISCOPAL CHURCH
79 6th Street
www.mytrinitychurch.org

This church is believed to be one of the first prefabricated buildings in Florida, having been prepared in New York and sent by ship to Apalachicola where it was assembled in 1837. During the Civil War, it is reported that the church bell was donated to the Confederate army to be melted for cannons, and the church carpets and cushions were made into army blankets.

Union army belt buckle. *(Maple Leaf collection, Image courtesy of the Florida Bureau of Archaeological Research and the U.S. Army)*
Union staff officer's button. *(Image courtesy of the Museum of Florida History)*

St. George Island

CAPE ST. GEORGE LIGHTHOUSE

St. George Lighthouse Park
201 East Gulf Beach Drive
850.927.7744
www.stgeorgelight.org

Completed in 1852 to replace the earlier 1848 lighthouse destroyed during a hurricane in 1851, the lighthouse was located at the southern tip of what is now Little St. George Island. At the beginning of the Civil War, Confederate authorities ordered the lighthouse darkened and in July 1861 arranged for the removal of the lighthouse lens for safekeeping. The lens and other equipment were taken to Apalachicola and then moved further inland to prevent its capture by Union forces. In December 1861, the USS *Hatteras*, on duty with the Gulf

Cape St. George Lighthouse, St. George Island.
(Image courtesy of St. George Lighthouse Association)

Blockading Squadron, landed a shore party at the lighthouse and found it abandoned. They used the lighthouse to observe Confederate shipping at Apalachicola, and Union sailors periodically returned for this purpose during the course of the war.

The lighthouse remained unlit until after the war when it was returned to service in August 1865. In 2005, shore erosion caused the lighthouse to collapse into the Gulf of Mexico. Using salvaged material from the collapsed lighthouse, the Cape St. George Lighthouse was reconstructed in the county park on St. George Island and reopened for public visitation in 2008. Reconstruction of the Keeper's Quarters for use as the lighthouse museum was completed in 2010.

Sumatra

FORT GADSDEN

Apalachicola National Forest
Forest Road 129-B
850.643.2282

Sited on the east bank of the Apalachicola River on Prospect Bluff, the known military use of this location dates back to the 1814 construction of a British post. After the British withdrew, it was occupied by some 300 blacks, many of them fugitive slaves. Viewed by the Americans as a haven for runaway slaves, a force led by Colonel Duncan Clinch, under orders from General Andrew Jackson, destroyed the "Negro Fort" and killed most of the occupants in July 1816 when a "hot shot" fired from a gunboat blew up the fort's magazine. Recognizing the strategic location of this site, General Jackson later directed Lieutenant James Gadsden to construct what became Fort Gadsden at the ruins of the earlier fort. Due to the significance of the Apalachicola River to area transportation, a company of Confederate infantry occupied this site in 1862 as a deterrent to Union navy ventures up the river. An outbreak of malaria in July 1863 forced the withdrawal of the infantry company, but a few Confederate sentries continued to be stationed at the fort for use as an observation post. In January 1865, several Confederate pickets at Fort Gadsden were surprised and captured by a Union navy raiding party. The Fort Gadsden site contains interpretative information in a kiosk building and on markers, including a State Historical Marker.

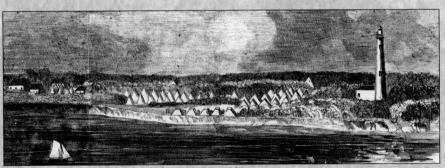

Pensacola Lighthouse and Confederate camp, 1861. *(Image courtesy of the State Archives of Florida)*

Lighthouses

At the time of the Civil War, there were 20 lighthouses and one lightship along Florida's shores. In 1861, most came under Confederate control, though those in the Keys and the Tortugas remained in Federal hands. Early in the war the Confederates extinguished the beacons under their management, so as not to be of use to Union vessels. At Jupiter Inlet, the keeper continued to operate the light until August 1861, when a group of Confederate sympathizers took control and removed its equipment. They then also disabled the Cape Florida Lighthouse.

Lighthouses that experienced significant military activity include the Egmont Key Lighthouse, the Cedar Keys Lighthouse, and the Pensacola Lighthouse which was damaged during an artillery bombardment in 1861. The St. Marks Lighthouse was the scene of much activity. It was shelled in 1862 and again in 1863, after which a Union landing party set fire to the lighthouse's wooden stairs. In 1865, a large Union force landed there prior to the Battle of Natural Bridge and retreated back to there after their defeat. After the war, as their lenses were found and other damage repaired, the lighthouses were relit, the last not until 1872, when a new lighthouse was built at Dames Point near Jacksonville to replace the lightship.

To learn more, see: *Florida's Lighthouses in the Civil War* by Neil E. Hurley, Middle River Press, 2007.

—— Gulf County ——

Port St. Joe

ST. JOSEPH SALTWORKS STATE HISTORICAL MARKER
1085 Cape San Blas Road

A State Historical Marker for the "St. Joseph Confederate Saltworks" is located just south of the site of a major Confederate saltworks that had a daily capacity of 150 bushels. Bricks for its foundations were salvaged from the nearby ruins of the City of St. Joseph, which had been abandoned due to yellow fever and a hurricane storm surge in the 1840s. In September 1862, the Union ship USS *Kingfisher* shelled the saltworks and sent a landing party ashore to destroy it. Prior to the bombardment, the ship's commander notified the Confederates under a flag of truce of his intentions and directed them to leave within two hours. The Confederates left in the allotted time, taking four cartloads of salt with them; there were no casualties.

Union Minie ball bullets.
(Maple Leaf collection, Image courtesy of the Florida Bureau of Archaeological Research)

—— Jackson County ——

Marianna

Battle of Marianna Monument, Marianna.
(Image courtesy of William Lees, Florida Public Archaeology Network)

During the Civil War, Marianna was an important trade center for products grown in the rich agricultural lands of Jackson County. The community also served as a Confederate military center with a training camp, hospital, storehouses, and government stables. In September 1864, a mounted Union force of 700 troops under the command of Brigadier

General Alexander Asboth conducted a raid deep into West Florida from their base at Pensacola. In the ensuing Battle of Marianna, the Union force routed the approximately 300 Confederate defenders consisting mostly of reserve forces and local Home Guard militia in a short but bitter engagement. (See the "Battle of Marianna" sidebar for more information.) After occupying Marianna and pillaging its buildings, the Union raiders withdrew back towards Pensacola the next day. A State Historical Marker for the "Battle of Marianna" is located on the Jackson County Courthouse Square. A second historical marker for the "Site of the Battle of Marianna" erected by the United Daughters of the Confederacy is located at the St. Luke's Episcopal Church. Two Confederate monuments are also located in Marianna. The first was constructed in 1881 and is located on the Jackson County Courthouse Square. The second monument was erected by the United Daughters of the Confederacy in 1921 in Confederate Memorial Park and commemorates the Battle of Marianna. Annual Marianna Day Civil War Reenactments, including a battle reenactment on the original Marianna battlefield, are held on the last weekend of September.

Battle of Marianna

In late 1863, Brigadier General Alexander Asboth took command at Pensacola of the Union's District of West Florida. He increased military operations and, in September 1864, decided to raid the town of Marianna, after receiving reports that it was being fortified and that Union prisoners were confined there.

The only force available to defend Marianna consisted of a few cavalry, as well as militia and troops home on leave. They barricaded the main street entering the town and waited for the Union attack, which came on September 27. The Confederates stopped the first charge, but Asboth led a second that proved more successful. The Confederate commander ordered a retreat, but many of the militia refused to abandon their town to the enemy. Fighting continued in the streets and in a cemetery, with some defenders trapped in the Episcopal church, which was set on fire by the Union troops. Low on ammunition, the remaining Confederate forces surrendered.

When the fighting ended, 10 Confederates lay dead or mortally wounded and 16 others wounded, with over 40 captured. Union losses were comparable with 8 dead or mortally wounded and 19 wounded, including General Asboth who suffered severe arm and facial injuries. By the time Confederate reinforcements arrived the next day, the Union force had departed and was well on its way back to Pensacola.

To learn more, see: *The Battle of Marianna, Florida* by Dale Cox, Published by the author, Expanded Edition, 2011.

Union Brigadier General Alexander Asboth.
(Image courtesy of The National Archives)

DAVIS-WEST HOUSE, CHIPOLA HISTORICAL TRUST MUSEUM
403 Putnam Street
850.482.3731

Constructed in c.1840 for local merchant John Davis, it became the home of Dr. Theophilus West upon his marriage to Davis' widowed daughter in March 1861. In May 1861, Dr. West enlisted in the 8th Florida Infantry, and in July 1862 was promoted to assistant surgeon. He served with the regiment in the eastern theater, and he was with the unit when the Confederate Army of Northern Virginia surrendered at Appomattox, Virginia in April 1865. In 1996, the house and its antique furnishings were willed to the Chipola Historical Trust for use as a meeting center and regional history museum.

ELY-CRIGLAR HOUSE HISTORICAL MARKER
242 West Lafayette Street

Erected by the Jackson County Historical Commission, this marker is located at the 1840 Ely-Criglar House. Ely Corner, which adjoined the house, was the scene of the initial fighting in the Battle of Marianna on September 27, 1864, when the attacking Union cavalry charged into the Confederate cavalry's line of battle. The first Union charge was driven back, but the second succeeded in forcing the Confederates to withdraw. Despite the fighting on the property, the house itself escaped major damage. The house is privately owned and is not open for tours.

HOLDEN HOUSE HISTORICAL MARKER
217 West Lafayette Street

Erected by the Chipola Historical Trust, this marker is located at the 1850 Holden House. The house was the residence of William E. Anderson who was a brigadier general in the Florida militia before the Civil War. Captured during the Battle of Marianna while serving with the Home Guards, he identified himself as a "brigadier general" and was imprisoned with other Confederate officers at New Orleans, Fort Lafayette in New York, and Fort Warren in Massachusetts. He was released from the latter prison on June 26, 1865, after signing an affidavit verifying that he had never held the rank of brigadier general in the service of the Confederacy. The building was briefly occupied by Union troops after the Battle of Marianna and presumably looted, but was not destroyed. The house was also the post-war residence of Dr. Julius T. Holden, surgeon of the 6th Florida Infantry from 1862 until his surrender at Durham Station, North Carolina in April 1865. The house is privately owned and is not open for tours.

RIVERSIDE CEMETERY
Bertram and Franklin Streets

This cemetery contains the remains of at least 42 Confederate veterans, including Dr. Theophilus West, the assistant surgeon of the 8th Florida Infantry in the Army of Northern Virginia, and several soldiers who participated in the Battle of Marianna. Union casualties from the Battle of Marianna were also buried here but their remains were relocated to the Barrancas National Cemetery at Pensacola after the war.

African Americans

Africans have been associated with Florida since the first Spanish exploration in 1513, with the first known enslaved Africans being brought to the colony in 1528. By the mid-1800s, parts of Florida had developed a system of plantation agriculture similar to the more populous slave states. This led to an increase in the number of slaves brought southward, primarily to work on the farms and plantations in the northern part of the state. In 1860, the African American population of Florida comprised nearly 45 percent of the state's population. Less than 1,000 free blacks resided in the state, along with 61,745 enslaved persons.

Emancipated slaves in front of Provost Marshal's Office in Jacksonville, c.1864. *(Image courtesy of The National Archives)*

At the war's outbreak, a few slaves accompanied their owners into the military, serving as body servants and cooks. A small number of slaves served as musicians in units like the St. Augustine Blues. The great majority of Florida's slaves remained on the plantations and farms providing, however unwillingly, the food needed to supply rebel armies. Confederate officials also impressed slaves to build fortifications and work on other war-related projects.

By early 1862, Union forces had occupied most of the populous towns along the Atlantic and Gulf coasts. These enclaves attracted hundreds of escaped slaves, and their numbers only increased as the war progressed. Many ships in the East Gulf Blockading Squadron enlisted escaped slaves into their crews, and more than 1,000 black Floridians joined Union army regiments. Even those slaves who remained in Confederate-held areas became more belligerent as the war progressed, as they sensed the Confederacy's defeat and slavery's demise. May 20, the day Union forces in Tallahassee announced the Emancipation Proclamation in 1865, is still celebrated by Florida's black citizens as Emancipation Day.

To learn more, see: *Slavery in Florida: Territorial Days to Emancipation* by Larry Eugene Rivers, University Press of Florida, 2000.

ST. LUKE'S CEMETERY

4362 East Lafayette Street

This cemetery was the scene of the culmination of the Battle of Marianna on September 27, 1864, when Union troops defeated Confederate forces, consisting mainly of Marianna Home Guard militia, during fighting among the graves. The adjacent St. Luke's Episcopal Church was burned by Union troops during the battle. Rebuilt twice after the Civil War, the present church building displays the original pulpit Bible in a glass case which, according to local tradition, was saved from the burning church by Union Major Nathan Cutler of the 2nd Maine Cavalry. The cemetery contains the remains of 40 Southern officials and soldiers, including Florida Civil War Governor John Milton, Confederate District Court Judge George S. Hawkins, Confederate Army Surgeon Dr. Julius T. Holden, and several Confederate soldiers who participated in the Battle of Marianna.

—— Liberty County ——
Bristol

TORREYA STATE PARK

2576 NW Torreya Park Road
850.643.2674
www.floridastateparks.org/torreya

Located high above the eastern bank of the Apalachicola River, a Confederate battery of three paired gun emplacements located in the present-day park property protected this vital waterway. Consisting of six heavy cannons ranging in size from 18-pounders to 32-pounders mounted on raised firing platforms and linked by

Gregory House, Torreya State Park.
(Image courtesy of the Florida Park Service)

communication trenches, this battery was constructed on Battery Bluff (also known as Neal's Bluff) in 1863. The remains of the battery earthworks and connecting trenches are located along the park's bluff walking trail, and the six gun emplacements are marked with signage. Another sign at the site provides a brief history of the Confederate battery. The Gregory House, built in 1849, was originally located on the western bank of the river at Ocheesee Landing. Some of the sailors injured by the boiler explosion on the Confederate gunboat CSS *Chattahoochee* in May 1863 were cared for at the house. In 1935, the Gregory House was dismantled, moved across the river and reconstructed at this site by the New Deal's Civilian Conservation Corps. The house contains period furnishings, including the Civil War era trunk of Captain William T. Gregory, who was a delegate to the Florida Secession Convention and then served in the 5th Florida Infantry. Captain Gregory was badly wounded at the Battle of Antietam (Sharpsburg), Maryland in September 1862. After spending nearly one month in a military hospital, he was given a medical furlough to return home and died at his residence in December 1862.

—— Okaloosa County ——
Fort Walton Beach

FORT WALTON BEACH HERITAGE PARK & CULTURAL CENTER

139 Miracle Strip Parkway Southeast
850.833.9595
www.fwb.org/index.php/museums.html

This city park includes the prehistoric Fort Walton Temple Mound, the Indian Temple Mound Museum, and two early 20th century historic structures. In April 1861, the local Confederate military unit, the Walton Guards, established Camp Walton at the base of the massive temple mound and used its top as a post for observing the movement of Union ships in the Gulf of Mexico. In March 1862, troops

Confederate cannon, Fort Walton Beach.
(Image courtesy of William Lees, Florida Public Archaeology Network)

from Camp Walton skirmished with a landing force of Union sailors at East Pass (present day Destin). In the ensuing fight, the Union force suffered two dead and two wounded while the Confederate force suffered no serious casualties. In response, a small Union force from Fort Pickens shelled Camp Walton from Santa Rosa Island in April 1862. Although camp buildings were destroyed by fire, no casualties were reported. To defend Camp Walton against future attacks, Confederate General Braxton Bragg had an 18-pounder carronade cannon moved to the camp from Fort Barrancas in Pensacola. In August 1862, Camp Walton was abandoned and the troops sent to the Army of Tennessee as part of the 1st Florida Infantry. The cannon was disabled and buried in a prehistoric shell mound. Discovered in the 1930s, the artillery piece was first displayed at the nearby Indianola Inn until the hotel burned down in 1962. The cannon was then moved to the outside of the Indian Temple Mound Museum, where it is now on display. The museum also houses a Civil War exhibit with period artifacts which is scheduled to be moved to a newly-constructed building at the center. Two State Historical Markers for "Fort Walton" and the "Indianola Inn, an Indian Midden Mound, and Civil War Cannons" contain information on the history of Camp Walton.

Confederate Major General
James Patton Anderson.
(Image courtesy of the State Archives of Florida)

Florida Confederate Generals

In addition to Joseph Finegan and Edmund Kirby Smith (see pages 46 and 50), a number of other Confederate general officers were either born or raised in Florida or closely associated with the state.

• James Patton Anderson, of Monticello, served as colonel of the 1st Florida Infantry before being promoted to brigadier general in 1862 and then major general in 1864. He commanded a division in the Army of Tennessee and also for a time the District of Florida.

• Theodore W. Brevard, of Tallahassee, served as colonel of the 11th Florida Infantry. In March 1865, he was commissioned brigadier general, the last general officer of the war appointed by President Jefferson Davis, and commanded the Florida Brigade of the Army of Northern Virginia.

• Robert Bullock, of Ocala, served as colonel of the 7th Florida Infantry in the Army of Tennessee and for a time commanded its Florida Brigade. In 1864, he was promoted to brigadier general.

• William G.M. Davis, of Apalachicola, served as colonel of the 1st Florida Cavalry. Promoted to brigadier general in 1862, he commanded the Department of East Tennessee. Davis resigned in 1863 and subsequently operated blockade runners from North Carolina.

• Jesse Johnson Finley, of Marianna, served as colonel of the 6th Florida Infantry. Promoted to brigadier general in 1863, he commanded the Florida Brigade of the Army of Tennessee.

• William Wing Loring, a career soldier raised in St. Augustine, was commissioned a brigadier general in 1861 and major general in 1862. Loring served in both the eastern and western theaters as a division commander.

• James McQueen McIntosh, a West Point graduate born in Tampa, was promoted from colonel to brigadier general in 1862. He was killed at the Battle of Pea Ridge (Elkhorn Tavern), Arkansas in March 1862.

• William Miller, of Milton, served as colonel of the 1st Florida Infantry in the Army of Tennessee. He was promoted to brigadier general in 1864, commanded the District of Florida, and was the Confederate field commander at the Battle of Natural Bridge in March 1865.

• Edward A. Perry, of Pensacola, became brigadier general in August 1862 and commanded the Florida Brigade in the Army of Northern Virginia until 1864. Perry was elected Florida governor in 1884.

• Francis A. Shoup, of St. Augustine, was appointed brigadier general in 1862 and served in both the western and eastern theaters as an artillery and staff officer.

• Martin L. Smith, chief engineer for the Florida Railroad, was promoted to brigadier general and then major general in 1862, and served as chief of the Confederate Corps of Engineers.

To learn more, see: *Generals in Gray* by Ezra J. Warner, Louisiana State University Press, 1959.

Confederate Major General
William Wing Loring.
(Image courtesy of the State Archives of Florida)

— Santa Rosa County —

Bagdad

When the Civil War began, Bagdad was an important West Florida center for the lumbering and naval stores industries with a large lumber mill complex and a shipyard. In early 1862, the Confederate government began withdrawing troops from the Pensacola Bay area to reinforce their forces in Tennessee. As part of this evacuation in March 1862, a detachment of the 1st Florida Infantry set fire to the lumber operations and shipyard in order to prevent their falling into Union hands. The fire inadvertently spread out of control and destroyed a number of adjacent homes. Most of the residents fled to Confederate held areas in the vicinity of Greenville, Alabama. Throughout the war, Union forces periodically conducted raiding expeditions into Santa Rosa County from their base at Pensacola. During a series of raids in October 1864, Union forces fought a skirmish with Confederate troops south of Bagdad and then briefly occupied the community.

BAGDAD CEMETERY
Pooley Street
850.623.9939
www.bagdadcemetery.com

This cemetery contains the remains of at least 15 Confederate and Union military veterans. Also buried here is Martin F. Bruce, a partner in the Bagdad shipbuilding firm of Ollinger & Bruce which, during the Civil War, was contracted to build a 110-foot gunboat for the Confederate States Navy. The vessel never saw service, as it was scuttled during the Confederate evacuation from Bagdad in March 1862 to prevent it from falling into Union hands.

BAGDAD VILLAGE MUSEUM & COMPLEX
4512 Church Street
850.983.3005
www.bagdadvillage.org

Housed in the restored c.1886 New Providence Missionary Baptist Church building, the Bagdad Village Preservation Association Museum contains exhibits on local history including a Civil War exhibit with period artifacts and photographs.

THOMPSON HOUSE AND CIVIL WAR SKIRMISH STATE HISTORICAL MARKER
4620 Forsyth Street

A double-sided State Historical Marker for "The Thompson House" and the "Skirmish on the Blackwater" provides information on the c.1847 Thompson House and on the October 1864 Union raids in the area. The house was the residence of Benjamin W. Thompson, a partner in the lumbering firm of E.E. Simpson and Company. Two of his sons, Oliver Thompson and Benjamin W. Thompson, Jr., served in the 1st Florida Infantry which fought in the western theater, and both were killed during the war. The Thompson House was occupied by Union forces during an October 1864 raid on Bagdad and Milton. Lieutenant Colonel Andrew B. Spurling of the 2nd Maine Cavalry commanded the Union raiding force which included the 1st Florida Union Cavalry, a regiment formed of Southern Unionist refugees and Confederate deserters. Spurling would later go on to receive the Medal of Honor for his actions during a Union raid at Evergreen, Alabama in March 1865. During a restoration of the house in 1976, two instances of graffiti with drawings and signatures which had been scratched on the plaster walls by Union troops and later covered with wallpaper were uncovered. One message in the drawing room stated "Bagdad Mr. Tompson [sic] Spurling First Fla Cavalry camped in your house the 26th of Oct 1864." A similar message dated October 28, 1864 was uncovered on the wall of the upstairs cross hall written by a different individual. The house is privately owned but is occasionally open to the public during the Bagdad Village Preservation Association's Blackwater Heritage Tour of Historic Homes.

Milton

ARCADIA MILL SITE
5709 Mill Pond Lane
850.626.3084
www.historicpensacola.org/arcadia.cfm

Florida's largest antebellum industrial complex, the Arcadia Mill was the site of a water-powered business that included a sawmill, lumber mill, gristmill, shingle mill, cotton textile mill, and bucket and pail factory. The facility was in operation from 1830 to 1855 when the two-story textile mill burned. The complex included a dam over a quarter of a mile long and about 15 feet high, which formed a 160-acre man-made pond for holding hewn timber and controlling the flow of water to the mills. During the Civil War, several skirmishes were fought in the Arcadia Mill area between Union raiders from Pensacola and local Confederate defenders, and a small Confederate cavalry force frequently used it as its base. Although the mill facilities were abandoned after the 1855 fire, the large dam remained and appears to have been destroyed by the Confederates during the war in order to prevent any use of the site by Union forces. Arcadia Mill contains a visitor center and museum, and an elevated boardwalk through the archaeological remains.

—— Walton County ——

DeFuniak Springs

CONFEDERATE MONUMENT
100 East Nelson Avenue
Located on the lawn of the county courthouse, the Walton County Confederate monument is apparently

Confederate Monument, DeFuniak Springs.
(Image courtesy of William Lees, Florida Public Archaeology Network)

Florida's first stone memorial to the Confederacy. The monument was originally erected in 1871 at the Euchee Valley Presbyterian Church by the Walton County Female Memorial Association at a cost of $250. It was subsequently moved to the county seat of Eucheeanna, which was the site of a skirmish during the 1864 Union expedition against Marianna. The monument was finally moved to DeFuniak Springs after that community became the new county seat in 1886. The monument lists the names of 94 Confederate war dead from Walton County. A State Historical Marker for "Florida's First Confederate Monument" is located on the courthouse grounds.

——Washington County——

Vernon

MOSS HILL UNITED METHODIST CHURCH
Corner of Vernon and Greenhead Roads
Three Miles Southeast of Vernon

Constructed in 1857 by church members and their slaves, the wood-framed Moss Hill United Methodist Church in the Holmes Valley is an excellent example of Florida frontier church architecture. In September 1864, the Vernon Home Guard under the command of Captain W.B. Jones, which contained members of the Moss Hill Church congregation, was called out when a Union force attacked Marianna in Jackson County. Riding to their neighboring city's assistance, the Home Guard unit unexpectedly encountered the Union army column commanded by Brigadier General Alexander Asboth returning from Marianna. In the ensuing skirmish known as the "Battle of Vernon", the numerically superior Union force routed the outnumbered Home Guard, killing one Confederate and capturing several more, including Captain Jones. In the Moss Hill Cemetery adjacent to the church building are the remains of at least 20 Confederate veterans including members of the Vernon Home Guard. A State Historical Marker for "Moss Hill" is located at the church site.

—— Alachua County ——

Archer

COTTON WOOD PLANTATION STATE HISTORICAL MARKER
State Road 346 (High Street)

A State Historical Marker for "David Yulee and Cotton Wood Plantation" is located about one mile southwest of the location of Yulee's plantation. David Levy Yulee was the developer of the Florida Railroad and was serving as United States Senator when Florida seceded from the Union. He resigned his Senate seat and returned to Florida during the Civil War to devote time to his plantations and his railroad. After the destruction of his Margarita Plantation at Homosassa by Union troops in 1864, Yulee and his family spent the remainder of the war at his Cotton Wood Plantation. Upon the fall of the Confederacy, the baggage train of President Jefferson Davis, including official documents and the slim remnants of the Confederate treasury, reached Cotton Wood Plantation in May 1865. Davis had been captured in Georgia earlier that month and his baggage train contents were kept hidden at Cotton Wood Plantation until they were sent to the stationmaster at Waldo, where they were seized by Union troops in June 1865. Yulee's Cotton Wood Plantation home was destroyed in the late 1970s or early 1980s.

Gainesville

By the time of the Civil War, Gainesville was an important stop on the Florida Railroad, which ran from Fernandina to Cedar Key, for the transportation of cotton and foodstuffs from the region's rich agricultural lands and cattle from South Florida. It was also a center for commercial lumbering mills. During the war, it gained added significance as a supply depot for the Confederacy. Gainesville was the scene of two military engagements during the Civil War. In February 1864, a Union force of 50 men left their encampment at Sanderson for Gainesville in an attempt to capture or destroy railroad trains that were believed to be there. They occupied Gainesville for over two days and skirmished with a small Confederate force before returning to Sanderson after destroying Confederate supplies. In August 1864, a larger Union force of 340 men under the command of Colonel Andrew Harris entered Gainesville where they were attacked by a Confederate force of 175 men commanded by Captain J.J. Dickison. In the ensuing battle, the Union force was completely routed with 200 casualties, the majority of which were captured. The Confederate force suffered less than 10 killed or wounded. A double-sided State Historical Marker for the "First Gainesville Skirmish/Battle of Gainesville" is located on the Gainesville City Hall lawn and provides details on these actions. In 1904, the United Daughters of the Confederacy erected a Confederate monument in Gainesville, which is located on the Alachua County Administration Building grounds.

BAILEY HOUSE STATE HISTORICAL MARKER
1121 NW 6th Street

A State Historical Marker is located at the c.1850 Bailey House, the home of James B. Bailey, a member of the Alachua County Central Committee which coordinated local mobilization for the Civil War. During the war, Bailey served the Confederacy as Superintendent of

Battle of Gainesville, August 1864, from *Dickison and His Men*. *(Image courtesy of the State Archives of Florida)*

Labor for the Engineers Department of the Florida Eastern District. He died while working on the fortifications at Baldwin in 1864. His eldest son, Casermo O. Bailey, served in both the 7th Florida Infantry in the western theater and the 9th Florida Infantry in the eastern theater and was also wounded at the 1864 Battle of Olustee in Florida. The house is currently used as a retirement center and is not open for tours.

EVERGREEN CEMETERY
401 SE 21st Street

This cemetery contains the remains of at least 65 Confederate veterans and at least three Union veterans. Confederate graves include those of Robert W. Davis, who was a veteran of the 5th Georgia Infantry, a U.S. Congressman from Florida and Mayor of Gainesville in the postwar period, and Brigadier General Jesse J. Finley, who commanded Florida troops in the Army of Tennessee in the western theater and was also a U.S. Congressman from Florida in the postwar period. A State Historical Marker for "Jesse Johnson Finley" is located in the cemetery.

HAILE HOMESTEAD AT KANAPAHA PLANTATION
8500 SW Archer Road
352.336.9096
www.hailehomestead.org

The Thomas Evans Haile family moved from Camden, South Carolina to this site in 1854 to establish a 1,500-acre Sea Island cotton plantation which they named Kanapaha. Built by enslaved black craftsmen, the main house was completed in 1856. During the Civil War, Thomas E. Haile served as a lieutenant in the 2nd Florida Cavalry and his oldest son, John, enlisted as a private. In May 1865, a month after the capture of Richmond by Union forces, the baggage train of President Jefferson Davis reached Alachua County. Upon hearing that Davis had been captured in Georgia earlier in the month, members of the small baggage train guard hid its contents at David Levy Yulee's Cotton Wood Plantation at Archer and sought parole from Union forces. Two of these men, Sid Winder and Francis Trench Tilghman, who left a diary of the events,

were provided shelter at Kanapaha before proceeding to Jacksonville to surrender. The Hailes had the unusual habit of writing on the walls of their home, and over 12,500 words, with the oldest dating to the 1850s, are visible in almost every room and closet of the main house.

MATHESON MUSEUM COMPLEX
513 East University Avenue
352.378.2280
www.mathesonmuseum.org

This complex includes the Matheson Museum housed in the 1930s American Legion Hall and the 1867 Matheson House. The museum contains permanent and temporary exhibits on Alachua County history, including a Civil War exhibit with documents, photographs and period artifacts. The museum also houses a research library and archives with an extensive collection of papers, books, periodicals, maps, photographs, postcards and other documents.

OLD GAINESVILLE DEPOT
Depot Avenue

A portion of this building was constructed in c.1860. It is the only remaining Civil War railroad depot from the Florida Railroad line which ran from Fernandina to Cedar Key. During the Battle of Gainesville on August 17, 1864, Union troops took up positions along the railroad and in the depot, and were driven out by the Confederate forces. It is one of only three known surviving Florida Civil War railroad depots, the other two being located on the Pensacola & Georgia Railroad line.

Florida railroad currency note, 1863. *(Image courtesy of the State Archives of Florida)*

Railroads

At the time of the Civil War, major railroads in the state included the Florida Railroad, which ran from Fernandina on the Atlantic to Cedar Key on the Gulf; the Florida, Atlantic and Gulf Central, which ran from Jacksonville to Lake City; and the Pensacola and Georgia, which in 1861 completed a line from near Quincy to Lake City. Railroad mileage for the entire state totaled just 433, and important stretches had not yet been built. Also, the main Florida lines in the east had no direct connection with railroads in Georgia to the north.

In 1861, construction began on a connecting line between Lawton, Georgia, and Live Oak, Florida. The state government authorized the taking up of iron from David Levy Yulee's Florida Railroad to use for the Lawton to Live Oak connector. Yulee mounted a protracted legal campaign to protect his company's property. The Confederate government ultimately prevailed and the iron was removed from Yulee's line and used in the connector. The various delays, however, prevented completion until March 1865, just one month before the surrender at Appomattox and far too late for the railroad to have an economic or military impact.

To learn more, see: "The Florida Railroad Company in the Civil War" by Robert L. Clarke, *The Journal of Southern History,* Vol. 19, No. 2, May 1953.

P.K. YONGE LIBRARY OF FLORIDA HISTORY, UNIVERSITY OF FLORIDA

Smathers Library (Library East)
352.273.2755
http://web.uflib.ufl.edu/spec/pkyonge/index.html

The P.K. Yonge Library, in the George A. Smathers Libraries' Department of Special and Area Studies, is the state's preeminent Floridiana collection. It includes a diverse array of primary sources, and is the most comprehensive repository for early Florida newspapers. A core collection consists of the J. Patton Anderson Papers, which document the career of Confederate Major General James Patton Anderson, his military command in the West, Georgia, and Florida, and the fate of his family before, during, and after the war. Holdings also include his family papers and Civil War letters related to Florida and Floridians. The Library also contains numerous other letters, correspondence, diaries, papers and miscellaneous documents relating to the Civil War in Florida, including the letters of Confederate Secretary of the Navy Stephen R. Mallory, the David Levy Yulee Papers, and collections of letters from soldiers both Confederate and Union. The Library's Florida Historical Map Collection contains over 30 maps of Civil War Florida.

Women

While thousands of Florida men served on battlefields across the South, Florida's women performed a variety of roles on the home front. At the beginning of the conflict, they sewed uniforms and flags, prepared farewell suppers, and gave parties for departing troops. The state's female population also performed various activities to raise money for the war effort, and worked as nurses and matrons in hospitals established both in and outside the state. They dealt with shortages of most civilian products, both essential and luxury. The price of available items rose dramatically and the use of substitutes became commonplace.

With so many men serving in the Confederate armies, women played a greater role in the operation and administration of farms and plantations, undertaking many activities formerly considered the responsibility of men. Many female Floridians also endured the occupation of their towns and farms by Union soldiers.

Women corresponded with their loved ones in military service, and faced the possibility that their husbands, fathers, sons, and brothers might never return. "Bereavement", writes historian Tracy Revels, "stripped away the illusions of rapid, heroic

Ladies Soldiers Friend Sewing Society, Tallahassee, 1861.
(Image courtesy of the State Archives of Florida)

triumphs. . . . Unidentified remains and unknown graves tormented many grieving families. Mourning clothes were increasingly in short supply, [and] women comforted each other, urging widows and orphans to accept death as the will of God." The war's end brought sadness and despair for many white Florida women, but undoubtedly for some a sense of relief.

To learn more, see: *Grander in Her Daughters: Florida's Women During the Civil War* by Tracy Revels, University Press of South Carolina, 2004.

Micanopy/Rochelle

OAK RIDGE CEMETERY

County Road 234
Between Micanopy and Rochelle

This cemetery contains the remains of several Confederate veterans, including Madison Starke Perry, Governor of Florida from October 1857 to October 1861. Perry was a prosperous Alachua County plantation owner and staunch proponent of states rights. After the election of Abraham Lincoln as President in November 1860, Governor Perry urged the immediate withdrawal of Florida from the Union and called for a convention to consider secession. With the secession of Florida in January 1861, Governor Perry's administration oversaw the mobilization of Florida military units and authorized the seizure of Federal forts and arsenals in the state. After leaving office, Perry served as a colonel in the 7th Florida Infantry until illness forced his resignation in 1863. Perry died in March 1865 at his plantation home near Rochelle. A State Historical Marker for "Madison Starke Perry" is located at the cemetery.

Newberry

DUDLEY FARM HISTORIC STATE PARK

18730 West Newberry Road
352.472.1142
www.floridastateparks.org/dudleyfarm

This historic state park is a unique remaining example of a historic Florida farm from the mid-1800s. Located on a 333-acre site, this typical early Florida farm is comprised of 18 original buildings that served three generations of the Dudley family. The patriarch, Philip Benjamin Dudley, Sr., acquired this property in 1859 and constructed a double-pen, dog-trot log house before the Civil War. Dudley served as a captain in the Alachua Rangers, 7th Florida Infantry beginning in 1862, and likely saw service in Tennessee during this period. Discharged from the Confederate army in 1863 for health conditions, Dudley returned to Florida to operate his farm property. Artifacts on display in the park include the 1835 family Bible, which Dudley reportedly carried with him throughout his Civil War service.

Waldo

J. J. DICKISON AND DAVIS BAGGAGE TRAIN STATE HISTORICAL MARKER
State Road 24 in front of Caboose in City Park

A State Historical Marker for "Dickison and His Men/Jefferson Davis Baggage" is located in a city park in Waldo. Captain John J. Dickison of the 2nd Florida Calvary was known as the "Swamp Fox of the Confederacy" for his skill in defending the interior of Florida from Union raids and attacks. His forces often bivouacked at Camp Baker south of Waldo during the war. At the war's end in May 1865, Dickison and his men were paroled by Union forces and mustered out of service at Waldo. Also in May 1865, after the contents of Jefferson Davis' baggage train had been hidden on David Levy Yulee's Cotton Wood Plantation at Archer, Yulee had the chests and trunks containing the personal effects and papers sent to the railroad agent at Waldo, M. A. Williams, for safekeeping. In June 1865, Union troops of the 34th U.S. Colored Infantry under the command of Captain O. E. Bryant found them at Waldo. Captain Bryant confiscated the contents and sent them to Jacksonville where they were examined and then sent on to Washington, D.C.

— Bradford County —

Starke

CAPTAIN RICHARD BRADFORD STATE HISTORICAL MARKER
West Call and North Temple Streets

In March 1861, 15 days before Confederate batteries began firing on Fort Sumter in Charleston Harbor, Richard Bradford enlisted in the Confederate army at Madison. Less than seven months later, Bradford became the first Confederate officer from Florida to die in the Civil War. Captain Bradford was killed in October 1861 while leading his men of the 1st Florida Infantry during the Battle of Santa Rosa Island

Confederate Captain Richard Bradford.
(Image courtesy of the State Archives of Florida)

near Pensacola. Governor John Milton delivered the eulogy at his funeral in Tallahassee and, in December 1861, signed legislation changing the name of New River County to Bradford County in his honor.

— Columbia County —

Lake City

During the Civil War, Lake City served as an important Confederate transportation and supply depot center. The community was the eastern terminus of the Pensacola & Georgia Railroad from Tallahassee and the western terminus of the Florida, Atlantic & Gulf Central Railroad from Jacksonville. After the February 1864 Battle of Olustee, 13 miles to the east, scores of the more severely wounded, both Confederate and Union, were treated in Lake City hospitals and private dwellings. Union prisoners were kept there before being sent to other locations and eventually to the prison camp at Andersonville, Georgia. A large monument to the Confederate soldiers killed at the Battle of Olustee, erected in 1928, is located in the square in front of the Columbia County Courthouse in downtown Lake City.

LAKE CITY-COLUMBIA COUNTY HISTORICAL MUSEUM
157 SE Hernando Avenue
386.755.9096

This museum is housed in the restored c.1870 May Vinzant Perkins House. The house was the postwar residence of John Vinzant who served as a sergeant in the 1st Florida Cavalry which fought in the western theater. At the Third Battle of Murfreesboro, Tennessee in December 1864, Vinzant was so badly wounded that his right leg had to be amputated and he later spent several months as a prisoner of war at a Union camp at Louisville, Kentucky. After the war, Vinzant returned to Lake City and served as the Columbia County Clerk of the Circuit Court and County Tax Collector. In 1983, the house was acquired by the Historic Preservation Board of Lake City and Columbia County Inc. and the Blue-Grey Army Inc. to serve as their headquarters and as a museum of local history. The museum features Civil War uniforms, weapons, and other period artifacts and contains a research library relating to the history of Lake City.

Battle of Olustee Monument, Lake City.
(Image courtesy of William Lees, Florida Public Archaeology Network)

OAKLAWN CEMETERY
NW Matthew Street

This cemetery contains an Unknown Confederate Soldiers Area with the graves of 155 soldiers who were killed in the Battle of Olustee or who died in the Confederate hospital in 1864-1865, following the battle. The United Daughters of the Confederacy erected a large obelisk monument to the unknown soldiers at the site in 1901, and a small stone commemorative marker to the Confederate dead is located nearby. A small obelisk monument for Nena Moseley Feagle, the "Last Confederate War Widow of Florida" who died in 1985, is also located here. A memorial service is held at the cemetery in conjunction with the annual Olustee Battle Festival in February to honor those who died, both Confederate and Union.

—— Gadsden County ——
Chattahoochee

CHATTAHOOCHEE ARSENAL
100 North Main Street
850.663.7001
www.dcf.state.fl.us/facilities/fsh/about.shtml

Also known as the Mt. Vernon Arsenal (the community's early name) and the Apalachicola Arsenal (for the nearby river), the construction of the Chattahoochee Arsenal was authorized by Congress in 1832. Completed in 1839, the arsenal consisted of 17 buildings including officers quarters, barracks, magazines, business offices and a barn. With the exception of the magazines, the buildings were enclosed by a brick wall 12 feet high and 30

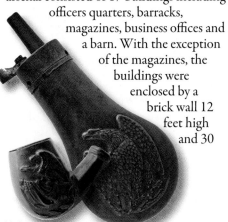

Union pipe bowl.
(Maple Leaf collection, Image courtesy of the Florida Bureau of Archaeological Research)
Gunpowder flask for small revolver.
(Image courtesy of the Museum of Florida History)

Chattahoochee Arsenal building, Chattahoochee.
(Image courtesy of William Lees, Florida Public Archaeology Network)

inches thick. In early January 1861, as the Secession Convention was meeting in Tallahassee, Governor Madison S. Perry ordered the seizure of the arsenal in Chattahoochee. On January 6, 1861, the local Gadsden County military unit, the Quincy Guards, seized the arsenal from a U.S. Army ordnance sergeant and his three man garrison without violence. At the time of its capture, the arsenal contained over 5,000 pounds of gunpowder, over 173,000 small arms cartridges, 57 flintlock muskets and one six-pounder cannon with over 300 shot and canisters. Throughout the Civil War, the arsenal was a center of Confederate military activity for regimental musters and training, as well as an arms depot. Following the Civil War, the arsenal was used by the Freedmen's Bureau from 1865 to 1868, and then as the state's first penitentiary until 1877 when it became the Florida Asylum for the Indigent Insane. In 1919, it received its present name, the Florida State Hospital, and continues to this day in use as a state mental institution. Two of the original arsenal buildings remain. The officers quarters is now used as the administration building for the hospital, and a magazine building is being rehabilitated for use as a museum and conference center.

CSS CHATTAHOOCHEE MONUMENT
South Main Street

The CSS *Chattahoochee* was a twin-screw steam gunboat which was built at Saffold, Georgia, and entered service in the Confederate navy in February 1863. The vessel patrolled the Chattahoochee and Apalachicola Rivers and often docked at the Chattahoochee Arsenal wharf. In May 1863, the ship suffered a horrific boiler explosion near Blountstown on

the Apalachicola River which killed or severely scalded many of her crew and disabled the ship. The dead sailors were taken to Chattahoochee where they were buried near the arsenal while the vessel was taken to Columbus, Georgia for repairs. During the Wilson's Raid campaign, when Union cavalry approached Columbus in April 1865, the ship was scuttled by the Confederates to prevent her capture. In the early 1960s, a 30-foot section of the stern hull and the steam engines were recovered and are now on display at the National Civil War Naval Museum in Columbus. In 1994, the United Daughters of the Confederacy erected a monument at the sailors' burial site in Chattahoochee which lists the names of the 17 sailors who perished in the explosion.

Quincy

Confederate Monument, Quincy.
(Image courtesy of William Lees, Florida Public Archaeology Network)

During the Civil War, Quincy was the location of the Confederate military headquarters for the Middle Florida District. Quincy also served as a Confederate commissary depot and hospital station with the Episcopal church, county courthouse, Quincy Academy and private homes used as make-shift medical centers after the Battles of Olustee and Natural Bridge. In 1884, a Confederate monument was erected in Quincy by the Gadsden County Ladies Memorial Association on the Gadsden County Courthouse Square.

A.K. ALLISON HOUSE
215 North Madison Street
850.875.2511 or toll-free 1.888.904.2511
www.allisonhouseinn.com

Constructed in 1843, this house was the residence of Abraham K. Allison, the Florida Senate President who became acting governor on April 1, 1865, after Governor John Milton committed suicide. Allison resigned the office on May 19, 1865, was arrested by Federal authorities, and in June was sent to Fort Pulaski, Georgia where he was imprisoned for several months along with other Confederate officials. Allison was also a delegate to the 1861 Florida Secession Convention and participated in the Battle of Natural Bridge with the state militia. The house is now operated as a bed and breakfast inn.

SMALLWOOD-WHITE HOUSE STATE HISTORICAL MARKER
**Corner of West King
and North Madison Streets**

A doubled-sided State Historical Marker for "The White House/Pleasants Woodson White" contains details on this house which was constructed in 1843 and remodeled to its present appearance in 1856. During the Civil War, this house was the residence of Pleasants W. White who served as a major in the Confederate army and as the Chief Commissary Officer for Florida. It was in the latter role that he issued the "White Circular" in 1863 appealing for desperately needed foodstuffs for the Confederate army. The depth of need for Florida foodstuffs and other supplies felt by the Confederate army was revealed to Union authorities when the circular found its way into their hands. Some contemporaries and historians believed that it influenced the Union's decision to mount a major expedition in Florida in 1864, which culminated in the Battle of Olustee. The house also served as the meeting place for the Ladies Aid Society which supported the Confederate cause with Mrs. Emily White as the chief organizer and president. Among their activities, this group of women tended to the injured and dying soldiers who

were brought to Quincy following the Battles of Olustee and Natural Bridge. The house is currently used as a church parsonage and is not open for tours.

Soldiers Cemetery, Quincy.
(Image courtesy of William Lees, Florida Public Archaeology Network)

SOLDIERS CEMETERY IN EASTERN CEMETERY
344 East Jefferson Street

This cemetery was established early in the Civil War for Confederate soldiers who had no family in Quincy and were too far from home for their bodies to be returned to their families. Located in the cemetery, a State Historical Marker for the "Soldiers Cemetery" provides information on the Civil War in Quincy, as well as the cemetery.

THE QUINCY ACADEMY STATE HISTORICAL MARKER
303 North Adams Street

A State Historical Marker is located at the building constructed in 1851 to house the Quincy Academy, a private educational institution for children of Gadsden and surrounding counties. During the Civil War, the building was used as a Confederate military hospital. The building is now used as a church community outreach facility.

WESTERN CEMETERY
King Street

This cemetery contains the remains of local Confederate soldiers and officials, including Dr. Thomas Y. Henry, the grandson of Revolutionary War patriot Patrick Henry, a delegate to the Florida Secession Convention and the Director of Confederate Medical Services for

West Florida. Also buried here is Edward C. Love, who was a delegate to the Florida Secession Convention and one of five commissioners (the most prominent being David Levy Yulee) appointed by Acting Governor Allison to negotiate with Federal authorities on behalf of Florida at the end of the war. Among the Confederate veterans buried here is William T. Stockton, a lieutenant colonel in the 1st Florida Cavalry. Stockton was captured at the 1863 Battle of Missionary Ridge in Tennessee and spent the remainder of the war as a Union prisoner of war at Johnson's Island in Ohio until his release in August 1865.

──Hamilton County──
White Springs

After the Union occupation of northeast Florida coastal regions in 1862, many residents of coastal communities fled inland to Confederate-held areas of the state. A number of these refugees came to White Springs, and the community became known as the "Rebel Refuge."

Confederate Lieutenant Robert W. Adams of White Springs.
(Image courtesy of the State Archives of Florida)

RIVERSIDE CEMETERY
Adams Memorial Drive

This cemetery contains the remains of local Confederate soldiers, including Robert W. Adams who served as a first lieutenant with the 5th Florida Infantry in the eastern theater including the Battle of Gettysburg, and later spent six months as a prisoner of war in a Union facility. After the war, Adams returned to White Springs where he became a prosperous merchant and community leader, and served in the Florida Senate.

— Jefferson County —

Lloyd

During the Civil War, Lloyd was an important stop on the Pensacola & Georgia Railroad, which ran from Lake City to Gee's Turnout near Quincy, for the transportation of Confederate soldiers and war materials as well as cotton and foodstuffs from Middle Florida's rich agricultural lands. After the February 1864 Battle of Olustee, some wounded Confederate soldiers were unloaded at the Lloyd Railroad Depot and treated in a make-shift hospital by local women in at least one private residence, the c.1855 Lloyd-Bond House. Two of their patients died and are buried on nearby Bond family land.

LLOYD RAILROAD DEPOT

State Road 59 and Lester Lawrence Road
http://gulfwindnrhs.org/Lloyd%20Depot.htm

One of the stations on the Pensacola & Georgia Railroad, the c.1858 Lloyd Depot was a center for trade and transportation in Jefferson County, including military usage for Confederate soldiers and war materials. It is one of only three known surviving Florida Civil War railroad depots.

Confederate soldier William Denham of Monticello.
(Image courtesy of the State Archives of Florida)

Monticello

During the Civil War, Monticello's function as a supply center was based on the rich Middle Florida agricultural lands of Jefferson County which produced cotton and foodstuffs, and on its manufacturing facilities. It was the site of a small shoe factory, a small woolen factory, and the Southern Rights Manufacturing Association's cotton mill which was the state's only cloth mill. Located a little over a mile east of the community, the cotton mill was known as the Bailey Cotton Mill for William Bailey, a Jefferson County planter and the major organizer and investor in the mill. It provided cloth, yarn, and thread to the Confederate commissary. During the war, Bailey refused to profiteer from the inflated prices caused by the Union blockade, and materials produced in the mill were sold to the Confederate government at the lowest possible rates. As a result, in the summer of 1864, Bailey and Florida Governor John Milton were able to convince the central Confederate government not to seize the cotton mill and its products as they had done with other manufacturing facilities. A spur of the Pensacola & Georgia Railroad was extended to Monticello in 1861. A Confederate monument was erected in Monticello by the Ladies Memorial Association in 1899 on the north lawn of the Jefferson County Courthouse.

OLD CITY AND ROSELAND CEMETERIES

North Waukeenah and East Madison Streets

Established in 1827, the Old City Cemetery is the oldest of Monticello's cemeteries, while the adjacent Roseland cemetery was established about 1850. These cemeteries contain the remains of local Confederate soldiers and officials, as well as some soldiers who were brought to Monticello and died there after being wounded at the Battle of Olustee. Among the Confederate veterans buried here is William S. Dilworth, a prominent Monticello attorney who was a delegate to the Florida Secession Convention and served as a colonel in the 3rd Florida Infantry. At one point early in the war, Colonel Dilworth commanded all troops in the Military District of East and Middle Florida. In May 1862, Colonel Dilworth and his unit were transferred out of Florida and the regiment served in the western theater until the end of the war, although Dilworth himself returned to Monticello in July 1864 on extended sick leave. Another Confederate veteran buried here is Samuel Pasco, who served in the 3rd Florida Infantry and was captured at the 1863 Battle

Lloyd Railroad Depot, Lloyd. *(Image courtesy of David Ferro, Gulf Wind Chapter, National Railway Historical Society)*

of Missionary Ridge in Tennessee. He spent the remainder of the war in a Union prison camp in Indiana before being paroled in 1865 as a sergeant. In the postwar period, Pasco was a state legislator and United States Senator; Pasco County, Florida was named in his honor in 1887. Also buried here is Smith Simkins, a lawyer and the first sheriff of Jefferson County, who manufactured salt for the Confederacy at various points along the county's Gulf Coast. Simkins was also one of the four members of the Florida Executive Council which met in 1862 to develop the state's war policies.

PALMER FAMILY GRAVEYARD AND PALMER-PERKINS HOUSE
625 West Palmer Mill Road

Owned by the City of Monticello, this cemetery is located adjacent to the c.1836 Palmer-Perkins House. Among those buried here is Dr. Thomas M. Palmer who was a delegate to the Florida Secession Convention and was appointed by Governor Milton as surgeon to the 2nd Florida Infantry. In 1862, he was appointed by Governor Milton as superintendent and director of the new Florida Hospital established in an old tobacco warehouse in Richmond, Virginia. At the end of 1863, the Florida Hospital was closed and Florida military patients were assigned to Florida wards at Howard's Grove Hospital near Richmond, where Palmer served as surgeon-in-charge until the end of the war. The house was most recently used as a bed and breakfast inn.

—— Leon County ——

Tallahassee

After Florida was ceded by Spain to the United States in 1821, Tallahassee was designated the capital of the new territory in 1824. Florida became a state in 1845 and, by the beginning of the Civil War, Tallahassee was a small but prosperous city in the center of Middle Florida's cotton plantation system, and an important transportation center. The community was the northern terminus of the Tallahassee Railroad, the state's first rail line, which ran to St. Marks and the western terminus of the Pensacola & Georgia Railroad which ran to Lake City. During the Civil War, the Pensacola & Georgia Railroad was extended westward to four miles east of Quincy at Gee's Turnout. Tallahassee was threatened with invasion in March 1865 when a Union force landed near the St. Marks Lighthouse and proceeded north toward the city. The initial objective was the capture of the blockade running port of St. Marks to the south, but Union commanders believed that a victory there could lead to the subsequent capture of Tallahassee and perhaps Thomasville, Georgia. The Union advance was halted at the Battle of Natural Bridge near Woodville about ten miles south of Tallahassee. In one of the last Confederate victories of the war, the Union force was compelled to retreat back to the coast. Tallahassee remained the only Southern state capital east of the Mississippi River not to be captured by the Union during the Civil War.

Militia and Home Guard

During the Civil War, Florida militia and home guard companies, comprised primarily of individuals either too old or too young, or otherwise unable to serve in the regular military, took an active role in a number of battles and campaigns.

The origins of the militia in Florida date from the Spanish period, making it the oldest in the present-day United States. When Florida left the Union, volunteer units occupied Federal installations in the state. Most of these volunteers were eventually mustered into Confederate units, leaving the state militia system in a shambles and, in early 1862, it was disbanded.

In 1864, the Confederate Congress authorized a new reserve force that led to the formation of the 1st Florida Reserves, which served until the war's end. In December, the state legislature passed the first militia law in two years, placing all males between 16 and 65 in state service. At this stage of the war, however, it appears unlikely that any formal organization of these men took place. Consequently, at late-war engagements like Marianna and Natural Bridge, the militia and home guard companies that took part were informal, ad hoc organizations. Nonetheless, they fought and sometimes died in defense of their state.

To learn more, see: *Florida's Army: Militia/State Troops/National Guard, 1565-1985* by Robert Hawk, Pineapple Press, Inc., 1986.

"Cow Cavalry" Florida Home Guard skirmish with Union cattle raiders.
(Artist: Jackson Walker, Image courtesy of the Legendary Florida Collection)

Bellevue (Murat House), Tallahassee Museum.
(Image courtesy of the Tallahassee Museum)

BELLEVUE (MURAT HOUSE)

3945 Museum Drive
850.576.1636
www.tallahasseemuseum.org

Now located at the Tallahassee Museum, the c.1840 Bellevue plantation house was moved in 1967 from its original location on Jackson Bluff Road in Tallahassee. From 1854 until 1867, Bellevue was the home of Catherine Murat, great grandniece of George Washington and the widow of French prince Achille Murat, who was a nephew of Napoleon Bonaparte. Murat was an ardent supporter of the Confederacy. Local tradition holds that, in January 1861, from the grounds of the Capitol building, she fired a cannon which announced that Florida had seceded from the Union. She was an active participant in the local Soldiers Aid Society which supported the Confederate cause. An important part of the war's home front, these societies often met several days a week in members' homes to sew clothing for soldiers, and received official recognition from the state government through legislative appropriations to purchase materials. Murat is reported to have provided food from her plantation for wounded Confederate soldiers receiving care in Tallahassee. The Bellevue Plantation exhibit at the Tallahassee Museum also contains the reconstructed kitchen house and a reconstructed slave cabin.

BROKAW-MCDOUGALL HOUSE

329 North Meridian Street
850.891.3900
www.talgov.com/parks/cc/brokaw.cfm

Constructed in c.1856, this house was the residence of Peres B. Brokaw, a Tallahassee businessman and political leader who served as the captain of a local militia unit, the Leon Cavalry. A supporter of secession, Brokaw led his troops in torchlight demonstrations during the January 1861 Florida Secession Convention, and served as a captain in the 2nd Florida Cavalry during the Civil War.

FLORIDA HISTORIC CAPITOL

400 South Monroe Street
850.487.1902
www.flhistoriccapitol.gov

Restored to its 1902 appearance in 1978-1982, the Old State Capitol building still retains at its core the original 1845 brick building. The Florida Secession Convention convened at this location and, on January 10, 1861, voted to secede from the Union. As Florida's Civil War capitol, Governor John Milton maintained his office at this site, and the building saw service as soldiers' quarters and an armory. On May 20, 1865, Union Brigadier General Edward McCook's forces formally raised the United States flag over the Florida Capitol building,

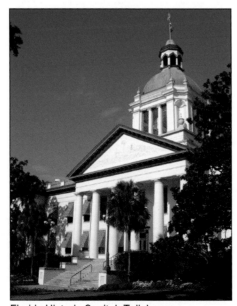

Florida Historic Capitol, Tallahassee.
(Image courtesy of William Lees, Florida Public Archaeology Network)

signifying Florida's official surrender. A new capitol building was built in the 1970s, and the restored Old State Capitol building opened in 1982 as a museum. It is now home to the Florida Legislative Research Center & Museum. Exhibits feature images, documents and military artifacts from the Civil War including an 1863 Union mountain howitzer with a gun carriage, and a replica of the flag believed to have been raised at the Capitol by General McCook. In 1881, a monument to Leon County Confederate soldiers was erected on the west side of the Capitol by a group of local women. In 1923, the monument was moved to its present location at the building's northeast corner.

FLORIDA STATE UNIVERSITY LIBRARIES SPECIAL COLLECTIONS AND ARCHIVES, STROZIER LIBRARY

116 Honors Way
850.644.5211
www.lib.fsu.edu/specialcollections

The University Libraries' Special Collections Department contains a variety of manuscript material relating to Florida in the Civil War. The collections include period letters, diaries, memoirs, family papers, official documents and correspondence, Confederate paper money, and other miscellaneous related items.

FORT HOUSTOUN

Old Fort Drive

Also known as the Old Fort, this earthen fortification is the only remnant of a number of earthworks constructed to protect Florida's capital during the Civil War. Probably constructed beginning in late 1864, the fort was sited on a hill in the southeast portion of the city on plantation property belonging to Edward Houstoun, and later by his son Patrick who commanded a Confederate artillery battery at the Battle of Natural Bridge. Due to their defeat at Natural Bridge, Union soldiers failed to reach Tallahassee to test this bulwark. In 1943, the property was donated to the City of Tallahassee. A State Historical Marker for "Old Fort Park" marks this good example of Civil War earthworks.

JACKSONVILLE, PENSACOLA & MOBILE RAILROAD COMPANY FREIGHT DEPOT

918 Railroad Avenue
www.trainweb.org/usarail/tallahassee.htm

Constructed in c.1858, a second story was added to the building by 1885. This depot was one of the stations on the Pensacola & Georgia Railroad and a center for trade and transportation in Leon County, including the transport of Confederate soldiers and war materials. Local tradition holds that the depot basement was used for the storage of Confederate munitions. It is one of only three known surviving Florida Civil War railroad depots. In 1869, the Pensacola & Georgia Railroad was purchased by, and consolidated with, the Jacksonville, Pensacola & Mobile Railroad.

KNOTT HOUSE MUSEUM

301 East Park Avenue
850.922.2459
www.museumoffloridahistory.com/about/sites

First occupied by Tallahassee attorney Thomas Hagner and wife Catherine Gamble, evidence suggests that free black George Proctor constructed this house in 1843. With the surrender of General Robert E. Lee's Army of Northern Virginia and General Joseph E. Johnston's Army of Tennessee in April 1865, Union troops arrived in Tallahassee on May 10. Brigadier General Edward M. McCook, commander of the Union force, briefly used this home as his headquarters. On May 20, 1865, McCook announced President Lincoln's Emancipation Proclamation from the house, declaring freedom for all slaves in the north Florida area. This event is commemorated each May 20 with a reenactment ceremony at the Knott House Museum. The house is interpreted to the period of the Knott family occupancy, 1928-1965, and a replica of McCook's headquarters flag is on display.

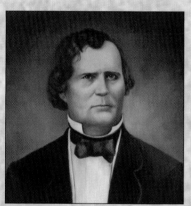

Governor Madison Starke Perry.
(Image courtesy of the Museum of Florida History)

Florida Governors in the Civil War

As the Civil War began, the governor of Florida was Madison Starke Perry of the Democratic Party. A South Carolina native, Perry settled in Alachua County in the 1840s, where he operated a plantation and became active in politics. In 1857, he ran against the American Party candidate for governor and won. Following President Lincoln's election, Perry asked the legislature to convene a secession convention, which in early January 1861 voted overwhelmingly for disunion. Perry guided the state during the critical period in which it left the Union and joined the new Confederate States of America. His primary goals were the occupation of U.S. government facilities in the state, the establishment of relations with the central government, and organization of the state's defenses.

After leaving the governorship, Perry helped organize the 7th Florida Infantry Regiment and, despite the fact that he had no prior military training or experience, was elected its colonel. The unit served in East Tennessee throughout Perry's tenure in command, though it experienced little combat until later in the war. The former governor resigned in June 1863 and returned home to Alachua County. He took no further active role in the war and died at his plantation in March 1865.

For most of the Civil War, the governor of Florida was John Milton of the Democratic Party. Milton was born in Georgia in 1807 and moved to Florida in the 1840s, where he operated a plantation in Jackson County. He also became active in politics, serving in the state legislature and leading the Florida delegation at the 1860 Democratic convention. Later that year, Milton defeated his Constitutional Unionist opponent in the gubernatorial election, and remained governor-elect for a full year. When finally assuming the duties of governor in October 1861, Milton faced a variety of problems arising from the war.

Early in his term, Milton's political opponents moved to limit the governor's authority, establishing an executive council to share power with the governor. He also faced a crisis when Confederate authorities withdrew most of the troops defending Florida, leading to the abandonment of parts of the state. Other issues facing Milton included the depletion of the state's finances, conscription, a growing Unionist sentiment in some areas, and the impressment of supplies by Confederate authorities. Though an ardent Southern nationalist, Milton criticized this seizure of property. Worn down by his duties and despondent over the imminent collapse of the Confederacy, Milton committed suicide on April 1, 1865.

With Milton's death, Senate President Abraham K. Allison of Quincy assumed the office of governor and presided over the state during the Confederacy's collapse. He resigned the office on May 19, 1865, was arrested by Federal authorities shortly afterward, and in June 1865 was imprisoned at Fort Pulaski, Georgia for several months along with other Confederate officials. Upon his release, he returned to Quincy, where he died in 1893.

To learn more, see: *The Florida Handbook, 2009-2010* by Allen Morris, Peninsular Publishing Company, 2009.

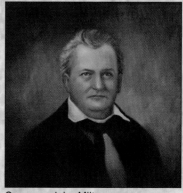

Governor John Milton.
(Image courtesy of the Museum of Florida History)

MEGINNIS-MUNROE HOUSE
125 North Gadsden Street
850.222.8800
www.lemoyne.org

Constructed in 1854, this house was moved southward on logs in 1903 to its present location, and is currently the home of the LeMoyne Center for the Visual Arts. During the Civil War, the house was used as a temporary hospital for Confederate soldiers wounded at the February 1864 Battle of Olustee.

MUSEUM OF FLORIDA HISTORY
R.A. Gray Building
500 South Bronough Street
850.245.6400
www.museumoffloridahistory.com

The Museum of Florida History collects, preserves, exhibits, and interprets evidence of past and present cultures in Florida. As the state history museum, it focuses on artifacts unique to the role Florida has played in America's history. A permanent Civil War exhibit includes selected military arms, soldier's personal items, home front artifacts, and original Florida unit flags. Highlights include: the flag of the Apalachicola Guards made by women early in the war, uniforms worn by Florida officers, the sword from a Floridian killed at the Battle of Shiloh, a slave impressment document from Alachua County, a howitzer and mortar,

the folding desk used by a Florida Union unit commander, a Confederate-made cavalry saber from Olustee, surgeons kits, a Union revolver found hidden in a wall of an old St. Augustine inn, and the flag of the 5th Florida Regiment carried at the Battle of Gettysburg. More information about the Civil War in Florida is found in the permanent exhibits section of the Museum's website.

OLD CITY CEMETERY
Martin Luther King Jr. Boulevard between Call Street and Park Avenue
850.891.8711
www.talgov.com/pm/occhist.cfm

Established by the Florida Territorial Council in 1829, this is the oldest public cemetery in Tallahassee, and was acquired by the City of Tallahassee in 1840. The cemetery contains both a Confederate soldiers section in the eastern half and a Union and Reconstruction soldiers section in the western half. At least 186 Confederate soldiers are buried in the cemetery with at least 55 in the Confederate section, and the rest throughout the cemetery in family plots. Notable among the Confederate veterans is Colonel David Lang, who commanded the Florida Brigade at the Battle of Gettysburg and the surrender at Appomattox. In the postwar period, he served as the Adjutant General of the Florida State Militia. A State Historical Marker for "Major General David Lang"

marks his gravesite. At least 72 Union soldiers, both black and white, are buried here, with at least 37 buried in the Union soldiers section, and the rest buried throughout the cemetery. It is said that some casualties from the 1865 Battle of Natural Bridge are buried in the Union section, although at least some of their remains appear to have been moved and reinterred in 1868 in the National Cemetery at Beaufort, South Carolina. Among the Union veterans buried in this cemetery is Major Edmund C. Weeks who commanded the 2nd Florida Union Cavalry, a regiment of Florida Unionists and Confederate deserters which operated out of Fort Myers and Cedar Key.

STATE ARCHIVES OF FLORIDA/STATE LIBRARY OF FLORIDA
R.A. Gray Building
500 South Bronough Street
850.245.6600
http://dlis.dos.state.fl.us/library

The Florida Collection in the State Library contains one of the most comprehensive holdings of Floridiana in the state. Books, manuscripts, maps, memorabilia, newspaper articles, and periodicals are among the 60,000 items in the collection. The State Archives of Florida is the central repository for state government documents. It is mandated by state law to collect, preserve, and make available for research the historically significant records of the state, as well as private manuscripts, local government records, photographs, and other materials that complement the official state records. Found in this collection are Confederate Pension Application Files, the Ordinance of Secession, correspondence, family papers and other valuable resources related to the Civil War in Florida. An online "Guide to Civil War Records at the State Archives of Florida" identifies and describes the many state, federal, and private Civil War records housed at the State Archives of Florida. The State Library's Florida Photographic Collection contains many images related to this period of Florida history, and are available to view through their website.

Museum of Florida History, Tallahassee. *(Image courtesy of the Museum of Florida History)*

ST. JOHNS EPISCOPAL CHURCH CEMETERY

M.L. King Boulevard and West Call Street

Established in 1840, this cemetery is the burial place for many of Leon County's most prominent families. Among those buried here is Theodore W. Brevard, who raised a Partisan Ranger Battalion at the beginning of the war that became part of the 11th Florida Infantry. In March 1865, Brevard was commissioned a brigadier general, the last general officer of the war appointed by Confederate President Jefferson Davis. He was captured at the Battle of Sailor's Creek, Virginia in April 1865 with half of the remnants of the Florida Brigade. Also buried here is Captain Patrick Houstoun, who commanded a Confederate artillery battery at the Battle of Natural Bridge; William D. Bloxham, who organized an infantry company from Leon County in 1862, commanded it throughout the Civil War and served two separate terms as Governor of Florida in the postwar period; and David S. Walker, who was appointed Governor of Florida by President Andrew Johnson in 1865 and governed the state during the first three years of Reconstruction.

TALLAHASSEE-ST. MARKS HISTORIC RAILROAD STATE TRAIL

850.245.2052

www.dep.state.fl.us/gwt/guide/regions/panhandleeast/trails/tallahassee_stmarks.htm

The first railroad chartered by the Florida territorial government in 1831, the Leon Railway Company became the Tallahassee Railroad Company in 1834, and was the first rail line to begin construction in the state. In 1837, the route between Tallahassee and the port of St. Marks was completed. The railroad served the Confederacy during the Civil War in the transportation of troops, supplies, and munitions between Tallahassee, Camp Leon, Camp Simkins, and St. Marks. Perhaps its greatest contribution came in March 1865, with the quick transport of troops from Tallahassee south to defensive positions at Natural Bridge. This timely arrival of men played a crucial role in the Confederate defeat of the invading Union force. In the 1980s, the rail line was abandoned and purchased by the State of Florida. The segment between Capital Circle and St. Marks became Florida's first state rail trail.

THE GROVE

100 West 1st Avenue

850.245.6300

http://flheritage.com/grove

Constructed in the 1830s, this house was the residence of Richard Keith Call, two-time Florida Territorial Governor and an ardent Unionist who openly and strongly opposed secession. When informed in January 1861 by jubilant secessionists that Florida had withdrawn from the Union, Call is said to have prophetically replied, "You have opened the gates of Hell, from which shall flow the curses of the damned which shall sink you to perdition!" Call died in 1862 at The Grove and was buried in the family cemetery behind the house. His daughter, Ellen Call Long, remained at The Grove during the Civil War while her son, Richard Call Long, served in the Confederate 2nd and 5th Florida Cavalry. In 1883, she published her historical memoir, *Florida Breezes,* which provides unique details of antebellum and Civil War events in Florida. Owned by the State of Florida, the property is undergoing restoration, and is scheduled to open to the public as an educational center and history museum in late 2012.

UNION BANK

219 Apalachee Parkway

850.599.3020

www.cis.famu.edu/BlackArchives/BlackArchivesAtUnionBank/index.html

Completed in 1841, the Union Bank is Florida's oldest surviving bank building. Chartered in 1833 as a planter's bank from which plantation owners could borrow against their land and slave holdings, it served as Florida's major Territorial Period bank. Crop failures, the Second Seminole War, and unsound banking practices led to the failure of the bank in 1843. The building reopened in 1868 as the National Freedman's Saving and Trust Company, serving emancipated slaves and refugees until 1874. Relocated to its present site from its original location near the southwest corner of Adams Street and Park Avenue in 1971, the restored building opened in 1984 as a museum. Now operated by Florida A&M University as a satellite facility of the Southeastern Regional Black Archives Research Center and Museum, the collection includes slavery-related artifacts and a rare State of Florida Civil War bond.

The Call-Collins House, "The Grove", Tallahassee. *(Image courtesy of the Florida Division of Historical Resources)*

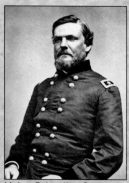

Woodville

NATURAL BRIDGE BATTLEFIELD HISTORIC STATE PARK
7502 Natural Bridge Road
850.922.6007
www.floridastateparks.org/naturalbridge

In March 1865, a Union force of approximately 1,000 troops, including two regiments of U.S. Colored Troops, under the command of Brigadier General John Newton, landed in the vicinity of the St. Marks Lighthouse for an expedition against the blockade running port of St. Marks and Fort Ward which protected it. Union commanders likely hoped that a victory there would lead in turn to the capture of Tallahassee and possibly Thomasville, Georgia. The

Union advance was halted at the Battle of Natural Bridge near Woodville, about 10 miles south of Tallahassee, by a hastily assembled Confederate force of some 1,000 men. The Confederate troops were a mixture of active duty troops and state militia, under the overall command of Major General Samuel Jones and on the battlefield by Brigadier General William Miller. Included among the Confederate troops was a small company of cadets from the West Florida Seminary, the predecessor to today's Florida State University. After their repulse by the Confederates, the Union troops retreated back to the coast for evacuation to their vessels. (See the "Battle of Natural Bridge" sidebar for more information.) In 1911, the United Daughters of the Confederacy (UDC) established a

Battle of Natural Bridge Monument,
Natural Bridge Battlefield.
(Image courtesy of William Lees, Florida Public Archaeology Network)

Battle of Natural Bridge

In February 1865, Brigadier General John Newton, Union commander of the District of Key West and Tortugas, proposed an operation to capture the small port of St. Marks, located on the Gulf coast south of Tallahassee. The plan was to land Union forces near the St. Marks Lighthouse, while a naval force ascended the St. Marks River to attack Fort Ward, a small Confederate fortification located there. If successful, it might have led to a movement to capture the Florida capital itself.

The expedition consisted of nine blockading ships, a number of transport vessels, and approximately 1,000 soldiers. The land forces were made up of elements of the 2nd and 99th U.S. Colored Infantry Regiments, and the dismounted 2nd Florida Union Cavalry. The troops began landing on March 4, 1865. The next day they

Union Brigadier General John Newton.
(Image courtesy of the State Archives of Florida)

skirmished with Confederates at East River Bridge and at Newport Bridge, where they hoped to cross the St. Marks River. Confederate Major General Samuel Jones had sent what troops he could muster under Brigadier General William Miller to resist the invasion.

Unable to cross at Newport, Newton learned of another point located over six miles to the north at Natural Bridge. Leaving the 2nd Florida Union Cavalry at Newport, he marched the black regiments to Natural Bridge. But the Confederates, using cavalry scouts, had anticipated the move. When the Federals arrived before daybreak on March 6, they found rebel forces already in position, with additional reinforcements steadily arriving. The Confederate defenders included infantry reserves, regular artillery and cavalry units, and assorted militia, along with a detachment of cadets from the West Florida Seminary (present-day Florida State University). The Confederates

Confederate Brigadier General William Miller.
(Image courtesy of the State Archives of Florida)

set up their troops in a large crescent-shaped line with converging fields of fire aimed at the crossing. The Southerners had a six-to-three advantage in cannons and held the high ground. During the day the Federals made several attempts to cross Natural Bridge, but were driven back by Confederate fire. Newton then withdrew his troops a short distance, where they repulsed an ill-advised but limited Confederate counterattack.

Unable to cross the St. Marks, he ordered a retreat back to the coast. The Union navy, meanwhile, had also been unsuccessful in its efforts to ascend the St. Marks River. The Navy did, however, award Medals of Honor to the six white sailors who manned their howitzers at Natural Bridge while serving with the Army expedition. Union casualties totaled 21 killed, 89 wounded and 38 captured or missing, while the Confederates suffered 3 killed and at least 23 wounded. The victory at Natural Bridge kept St. Marks and Tallahassee in Confederate hands until the conclusion of the war two months later.

To learn more, see: *The Battle of Natural Bridge, Florida: The Confederate Defense of Tallahassee* by Dale Cox, Published by the author, Expanded Edition, 2010.

committee to acquire title to the Natural Bridge Battlefield, and a land survey was commissioned. A portion of the battlefield was subsequently donated to the UDC which constituted the initial area of the present-day Natural Bridge Battlefield Historic State Park. In 1921, the Florida Legislature appropriated funding to assist the UDC in the construction of a monument at the site, and in 1922 a dedication ceremony was held at the completed monument. In 2000, a granite marker was installed behind the monument which lists the Confederate and Union soldiers who were killed in the battle or later died from their wounds. The UDC managed the property until 1950, when title to the six-acre site was transferred to the State of Florida. In 1970, the state acquired adjacent property of three more acres, and in 2009 an additional 55-acre parcel of the battlefield was acquired. Interpretive signage at the site describes the battle events. The Battle of Natural Bridge Reenactment, one of the largest such events in Florida, is held annually at the park in early March.

Union regiment reenactors,
Natural Bridge Battlefield.
(Image courtesy of Bruce Graetz, Museum of Florida History)

Civil War-era cannon at Cedar Key Museum State Park. *(Image courtesy of the Florida Park Service)*

—— Levy County ——
Cedar Key

At the beginning of the Civil War, Cedar Key was an important transportation center as a Gulf port city, and as the western terminus of the Florida Railroad from Fernandina. During the war, the Cedar Keys area was an active center for blockade running and salt production. In January 1862, a Union landing party from the USS *Hatteras* entered the town and destroyed the railroad depot and other buildings, the railroad wharf, railroad cars, several vessels, and the abandoned Confederate defenses. Most of the Confederate troops stationed at Cedar Key had been sent to Fernandina just days before in anticipation of a Union attack there. A small force of 23 men from the 4th Florida Infantry was left to defend the town, and 15 of them were taken prisoner while attempting to flee in a ferryboat; the remainder escaped. The town was blockaded by Union naval vessels of the East Gulf Blockading Squadron for the next two years. By 1864, Union forces had established a permanent military presence in the town and it became a base for conducting raids into the interior. During a return from one such raid in February 1865, a Union force of nearly 400 men from the 2nd U.S. Colored Infantry and the 2nd Florida Union Cavalry under the command of Major Edmund C. Weeks was attacked by a Confederate force of 145 men from several Florida units commanded by Captain J.J. Dickison at Station Four on the outskirts of Cedar Key. After a daylong fight, the Union force withdrew back into Cedar Key. Casualty reports differed, with Major Weeks reporting that he had lost 5 killed, 18 wounded and 3 taken prisoner and that the Confederates suffered at least 2 dead, while Captain Dickison reported total Union casualties of 70 and Confederate losses of just 5 men wounded.

CEDAR KEY HISTORICAL SOCIETY MUSEUM
609 2nd Street
352.543.5549
www.cedarkeymuseum.org

Located in the c.1871 Lutterloh Building, this museum contains an extensive collection of historic Cedar Keys photographs, documents and area artifacts. Displays include Civil War objects such as an inscribed wooden grave marker from Seahorse Key of a Union sailor who was killed in action in the area.

CEDAR KEY MUSEUM STATE PARK
12231 SW 166th Court
352.543.5350
www.floridastateparks.org/cedarkeymuseum

This state park contains the relocated 1890s St. Clair Whitman House and a museum building with exhibits featuring historic images and period artifacts on the history of the Cedar Keys area, including a Civil War exhibit. Two Civil War 24-pounder cannons, originally from Seahorse Key, and a Confederate salt kettle used for boiling sea water to produce salt are displayed on the museum grounds. Prior to its destruction during a Union raid in October 1862, the Cedar Keys saltworks had 60 kettles that could produce 150 bushels of salt per day.

OLD ISLAND HOTEL
373 2nd Street
352.543.5111
www.islandhotel-cedarkey.com

This building was constructed just prior to the Civil War in c.1859-1860 as the Parsons and Hale General Store. During the Civil War, one of the store owners, Captain John Parsons who had large property holdings at Bayport, raised and commanded two independent Home Guard companies from Hernando County for the defense of the region against Union raids. By the time of the Union occupation of Cedar Key, both store owners, Parsons and Francis Hale, had fled the city and the building is believed to have been confiscated for use as a Union barracks and warehouse. The building is now operated as a bed and breakfast inn.

Seahorse Key

CEDAR KEYS LIGHTHOUSE
Cedar Keys National Wildlife Refuge
352.493.0238
http://cedarkeys.fws.gov

The Cedar Keys Lighthouse was constructed in 1854 on Seahorse Key under the supervision of Lieutenant George G. Meade, who, in 1863, would command the Union Army of the Potomac at the Battle of Gettysburg. After the start of the Civil War in 1861, Confederate troops from the 4th Florida Infantry established a gun battery of three cannons on Seahorse Key, and the lighthouse lens was removed by Confederate authorities. In January 1862, the USS *Hatteras* was sent from the Union fleet at Key West to conduct a raid on the Cedar Keys. In addition to attacking Cedar Key and Depot Key, the raiders landed at Seahorse Key, which had been evacuated by the Confederate troops, and disabled the guns there to render them useless. In February 1862, a second Union warship, the USS *Tahoma*, returned to the area, shelled the gun emplacements on Seahorse Key, and sent ashore a landing party, which found the island again abandoned. In March 1863, Union sailors from the USS *Fort Henry* established a signal station at the lighthouse to keep watch for any Confederate shipping in the area. Seahorse Key was also used to house Confederate prisoners and Unionist refugees fleeing Confederate control during the remainder of the war. The lighthouse is currently used by the University of Florida as a Marine Science Laboratory, but is open to the public when the Cedar Keys National Wildlife Refuge holds open houses on Seahorse Key. Associated with the lighthouse is a small cemetery where four Union sailors are buried, two of whom were killed in action while the others died from illness and an accident. The remains of the gun battery are next to the graveyard in a small wooded area, and a brick powder magazine built during the Civil War is still standing adjacent to the lighthouse.

—— Madison County ——

Madison

Confederate Monument, Madison.
(Image courtesy of William Lees, Florida Public Archaeology Network)

During the Civil War, Madison was an important stop on the Pensacola & Georgia Railroad for the transportation of Confederate soldiers and war materials as well as cotton and foodstuffs from Middle Florida's rich agricultural lands. Several Confederate camps for the mustering and training of soldiers were located in the vicinity of Madison. In 1852, the Madison Shoe Factory was constructed 10 miles west of the town. It was the state's largest leather factory and annually produced 11,000 pairs of shoes, as well as wagon harnesses and other leather goods, for the Confederate government.

FOUR FREEDOMS PARK
Range and Base Streets

Erected in 1909 by the United Daughters of the Confederacy, a Confederate monument is located in Confederate Square in Four Freedoms Park. A plaque placed on the monument by the Sons of Confederate Veterans around 2005 lists the names of soldiers in units formed in Madison County who were "Killed in Action" and "Died in Service." The park also includes a monument erected in 1996 which is dedicated to the former slaves of Madison County.

OAKLAND CEMETERY
County Road 158

This cemetery contains the remains of at least 15 Confederate veterans and one Union veteran. Also buried here is John C. McGehee, a prosperous Madison County plantation owner and staunch proponent of states rights who was a delegate to the Florida Secession Convention in January 1861. He was chosen as president of the Convention and presided over its passage of the Ordinance of Secession. A State Historical Marker for "John C. McGehee" is located at the cemetery.

OAK RIDGE CEMETERY
601 NW Washington Street

This cemetery contains the remains of at least 105 Confederate soldiers and veterans. This includes the Confederate Section of the cemetery, which contains 31 graves with markers but no names. A State Historical Marker at the site for the "Madison Oak Ridge Cemetery" and a plaque on the cemetery's brick speaker's platform state that these 31 graves are the remains of Confederate soldiers killed at the Battle of Olustee.

TREASURES OF MADISON COUNTY MUSEUM AND MADISON COUNTY GENEALOGICAL LIBRARY

200 SW Range Avenue
850.973.3661
www.treasuresofmadisoncounty.com

Located in the restored 1890s W.T. Davis Building, these organizations promote the cultural heritage of Madison County through artifact, photographic, and genealogical collections. In their collections are copies of historic photographs, Civil War letters, and a journal from Madison County Confederate veterans.

WARDLAW-SMITH-GOZA HOUSE

103 North Washington Street
850.973.9432
www.nfcc.edu/community-programs/
wardlaw-smith-goza-conf-center

Prominent Madison County citizen, Benjamin F. Wardlaw, began construction of this house in 1860. The home served as a temporary hospital for Confederate and Union wounded following the Battle of Olustee in February 1864. In May 1865, Confederate Secretary of War John C. Breckenridge is reported to have spent the night here during his successful escape to Cuba while fleeing from Union forces at the end of the war. This historic house is presently used as a conference center by North Florida Community College. Tours are available.

— Suwannee County —

Live Oak

SUWANNEE RIVER STATE PARK

20815 County Road 132
386.362.2746
www.floridastateparks.org/suwanneeriver

In 1863, Confederate troops constructed earthenwork fortifications on a high bluff overlooking the junction where the Withlacoochee River joins the Suwannee River, a portion of which is preserved in this state park. These earthworks were constructed to protect the railroad bridge crossing the Suwannee River at the town of Columbus, a vital link in the cross-state transportation of troops and supplies. Destruction of this key bridge was one objective of the Union expedition into Florida in February 1864, which culminated in their defeat at the Battle of Olustee. The bridge was not threatened again for the duration of the war. The only extant remnant of the town of Columbus is the Columbus Cemetery which is also located within the park boundaries. The Confederate earthworks in the park can be viewed from a wooden walkway along the fortification. Interpretive signage provides information on historic sites within the park.

— Taylor County —

Perry

TAYLOR COUNTY SALTWORKS STATE HISTORICAL MARKER

US Highway 19 and County Road 361
Five miles south of Perry

With its 50-mile coastline and shallow coastal waters, Taylor County was a major center for Confederate salt production during the Civil War. Locations for saltworks in the region included Jonesville (present-day Adams Beach), the mouth of Blue Creek, the Aucilla River Slough, the mouth of the Fenholloway River, and Horseshoe Bay. The rugged terrain and sparse population of Taylor County made it a haven for Florida and Georgia Unionists and Confederate deserters who often joined together in armed bands and assisted Union forces in raiding the saltworks. During one such raid in February 1864, Union sailors from the USS *Tahoma* were assisted by nearly 100 of these men in destroying large saltworks described as being seven miles in extent. The raiders destroyed 6,000 bushels of salt, 390 salt kettles, over 280 buildings, and numerous other salt-making equipment and supplies. Additionally, over 1,000 cattle, mules, horses and wagons were captured and given to the Unionist and deserter band by the Union commander as the sailors returned to their ship. Despite the Union raids, salt-making operations continued in Taylor County for the duration of the war.

Confederate earthworks, Suwannee River State Park. *(Image courtesy of William Lees, Florida Public Archaeology Network)*

—— Wakulla County ——

Crawfordville

WAKULLA HISTORY MUSEUM & ARCHIVES

24 High Drive
850.926.1110
www.rootsweb.ancestry.com/~flwchs

Operated by the Wakulla County Historical Society, the museum and archives are located in the 1949 Old Wakulla County Jail building. The museum contains an exhibit on Roderick Donald McLeod, who served in the Confederate army's 7th Infantry Regiment, Georgia Reserves and moved to Wakulla County after the war. McLeod became very active in the United Confederate Veterans (UCV), the largest organization of Confederate veterans of the Civil War. The exhibit contains his Florida UCV memorabilia, documents, and memorabilia belonging to his daughter Martha McLeod who was very active in the United Daughters of the Confederacy.

St. Marks

FORT WARD, SAN MARCOS DE APALACHE HISTORIC STATE PARK

148 Old Fort Road
850.925.6216
www.floridastateparks.org/sanmarcos

Beginning in 1678, the Spanish built two wooden forts at the confluence of the St. Marks and Wakulla Rivers. In 1739, they began the construction of the permanent stone fort of San Marcos de Apalache. After General Andrew Jackson captured the Spanish strong point in 1818 and Spain subsequently ceded Florida to the United States in 1821, American troops intermittently occupied the fort, which they called Fort St. Marks. In 1857-1858, a federal marine hospital was constructed for the care of yellow fever victims. By the time of the Civil War, the fort had been abandoned. Confederate forces occupied the site in 1861, strengthened it with earthworks and artillery batteries, and renamed it Fort Ward. The fort provided

Ochlockonee River skirmish, 1863. *(Image courtesy of the State Archives of Florida)*

protection for both the small blockade running port of St. Marks and the town of Newport, which contained a foundry and several mills. A small Confederate steamer equipped with two cannons, the CSS *Spray*, assisted in the area's defense. Throughout the Civil War, the region was an active area for blockade running and salt production, and the Union navy had blockaded St. Marks since 1861. In July 1863, a Union navy expedition in small boats had attempted to move up the St. Marks River to capture Fort Ward and the CSS *Spray,* but withdrew when spotted by Confederate pickets. In March 1865, a much larger Union expedition with a major objective of capturing St. Marks and Fort Ward met with defeat at the Battle of Natural Bridge. Fort Ward remained in Confederate control until the end of the war when in May 1865 both the fort and the CSS *Spray* surrendered to a Union officer. The property was acquired by the State of Florida in 1964 for use as a park facility. A visitor center and museum, constructed on the foundation of the 1850s marine hospital, provides interpretation with exhibits and artifacts. An interpretive trail includes the Confederate earthworks and the highest point on the site, the Confederate powder magazine.

ST. MARKS LIGHTHOUSE

St. Marks Wildlife Refuge
County Road 59
850.925.6121
www.fws.gov/saintmarks/lighthouse.html

Constructed in 1842 to replace an earlier 1831 structure which was threatened by erosion, the St. Marks Lighthouse is located at the mouth of the St. Marks River on Apalachee Bay. After Florida

seceded from the Union in January 1861, the Confederates continued to operate the lighthouse until mid-1861, when authorities determined that it could not be secured against the Union navy, and removed the lens for safekeeping. In June 1861, Confederate forces erected a small artillery battery about 50 yards from the lighthouse which they named Fort Williams, and used the lighthouse for lookout purposes. In June 1862, Union navy ships shelled the lighthouse and sent ashore a landing party, which destroyed the evacuated Fort Williams and burned the lighthouse keeper's quarters. No casualties were reported for either side. In July 1863, the Union navy shelled the lighthouse again, and a landing party set fire to the wooden stairs of the lighthouse to prevent it from being used as a lookout post. In March 1865, approximately 1,000 Union troops landed in the vicinity of the lighthouse for an expedition against Newport, St. Marks and Fort Ward, which culminated in the Battle of Natural Bridge. After being repulsed by the Confederate forces, the Union troops retreated back to the lighthouse area where they reboarded their transport vessels. The lighthouse was relit with a new fourth-order Fresnel lens in January 1867.

St. Marks Lighthouse. *(Image courtesy of JV Marani)*

Battle of Olustee Reenactment. *(Image courtesy of William Lees, Florida Public Archaeology Network)*

—— Baker County ——

Olustee

OLUSTEE BATTLEFIELD HISTORIC STATE PARK

U.S. Highway 90
386.758.0400
www.floridastateparks.org/olusteebattlefield
http://battleofolustee.org

At the Battle of Olustee on February 20, 1864, Confederate soldiers turned back a Union thrust through Florida in the state's largest Civil War battle. Union Brigadier General Truman Seymour, with a force of approximately 5,000 soldiers, including a large number of U.S. Colored Troops, moved west from Jacksonville in mid-February with the aim of disrupting supplies from Florida to the Confederate armies and returning Florida to the Union in time for the 1864 Presidential election. Confederate Brigadier General Joseph Finegan, with reinforcements sent from Georgia by General Pierre G. T. Beauregard, met the invading force with an approximately equal number of troops east of Olustee. The ensuing bloody engagement was a clear Confederate victory, with Union soldiers retreating back to Jacksonville. (See the "Battle of Olustee" sidebar for more information.)

In 1899, the Florida Legislature authorized the erection of a monument at Olustee in recognition of the 1864 Confederate victory. In 1909, three acres of the battlefield were donated to the State of Florida, making it the oldest unit in the current Florida State Parks system. In 1912, with state funding assistance, a large monument was constructed at the site. The dedication ceremony drew over 4,000 participants, including many Civil War veterans. Smaller monuments were later erected near the main monument by the United Daughters of the Confederacy for Confederate Brigadier Generals Joseph Finegan, probably in the 1930s, and Alfred H. Colquitt in 1936. In 1991, a large granite cross monument was erected at the battlefield cemetery in honor of the Union dead of Olustee. The Olustee Battlefield Memorial was administered by the United Daughters of the Confederacy until 1949 when the Florida Board of Parks and Historic Memorials, the forerunner of today's Florida Park Service, assumed responsibility for it. The Florida Park Service manages an additional 688 adjacent acres of the battlefield owned by the U.S. Forest Service as part of the Olustee Battlefield Historic State Park. The park's visitor center contains exhibits with Civil War artifacts and interpretive panels that tell the story of the Battle of Olustee. A mile-long hiking trail through the battlefield contains interpretive signs that describe the events of the battle. The annual Battle of Olustee Reenactment, the largest Civil War reenactment in the state, is held during the second weekend in February at the park. A Civil War Expo also takes place here annually in September.

Battle of Olustee Monument, Olustee Battlefield.
(Image courtesy of William Lees, Florida Public Archaeology Network)

Battle of Olustee

Fought on February 20, 1864, the Battle of Olustee (also known as the Battle of Ocean Pond) was the largest Civil War engagement in Florida. Political and military considerations both played a role in the campaign's origins. Republican leaders hoped to see a loyal Florida government returned to the Union under the terms of President Lincoln's 1863 Reconstruction Proclamation, and to send delegates to the 1864 Republican presidential convention. Major General Quincy Gillmore, commanding the Union Army's Department of the South, hoped to prevent the flow of supplies to the Confederate armies and obtain recruits for the Union army's black regiments. About 6,000 troops were selected for the operation, with Brigadier General Truman Seymour in direct command. They occupied Jacksonville on February 7, and over the next several days mounted raids into the interior.

The Confederate commander of the District of East Florida was Brigadier General Joseph Finegan, with only about 1,500 troops. He called for reinforcements, which eventually brought the number of defenders to more than 5,000, and built a strong defensive position east of Lake City at Olustee. While the Confederates prepared, the Federal commanders bickered over their next movement. Seymour was pessimistic, believing that an advance on Lake City was not possible and that Unionist sentiment in Florida was less than the Federals had been led to believe.

1894 Lithograph of the Battle of Olustee. *(Image courtesy of the State Archives of Florida)*

Gillmore ordered that defensive works be constructed and that no advance be made westward without his consent. He then left Florida, returning to his headquarters in South Carolina. Seymour's confidence soon returned; he wrote that he now intended to advance to the Suwannee River to destroy a railroad bridge there. Gillmore dispatched an officer to stop the movement, but the Battle of Olustee occurred before he arrived.

Early on February 20, Seymour's army left Barbers Station for Lake City. When Finegan learned of the enemy's approach, he ordered his cavalry to draw the Federals towards his defenses. The fighting to the east intensified, however, and Finegan sent out additional troops to assist those already deployed. By mid-afternoon the skirmishing had escalated into a major battle. While Union Colonel Joseph Hawley positioned his brigade, a wrong command was given and one unit fell into confusion and quickly fell apart. This directed Southern attention

towards an untried black regiment, which occupied the Union left. It held the line for a time, suffering more than 300 casualties before retreating. With the destruction of Hawley's Brigade, Brigadier General Alfred Colquitt, in direct command of the Confederate attack, ordered a general advance. Seymour deployed another brigade to stop it, which stabilized the lines for a time.

The fighting during this phase of the battle was particularly severe. The Confederates captured several Union artillery pieces and threatened to flank the Federal infantry. By late afternoon, Seymour realized the battle was lost and sent forward his last reserves, the 35th U.S. Colored Infantry and the 54th Massachusetts, to protect a withdrawal. Many wounded and a large amount of equipment had to be abandoned. In the battle's aftermath, bands of Southern troops killed or mistreated some of the black Union soldiers left on the field. Fortunately for the Federals, the Confederate pursuit was poorly conducted, enabling most of their force to escape. The Federals suffered 1,861 killed, wounded, and missing in the battle, while rebel casualties numbered 946. The Olustee defeat ended Union efforts to organize a loyal Florida government in time for the 1864 election, though they did maintain their presence around Jacksonville for the remainder of the war.

To learn more, see: *Confederate Florida: The Road to Olustee* by William H. Nulty, University of Alabama Press, 1990.

Map of the Battle of Olustee (Ocean Pond). *(Image courtesy of the Museum of Florida History)*

Sanderson

SANDERSON CAMP STATE HISTORICAL MARKER
U.S. Highway 90

The text of the State Historical Marker for the "Camp at Sanderson" reads: This site was used by both Union and Confederate soldiers as a camp during the campaign of 1864. The camp was used as a Confederate supply depot but it was abandoned on February 9, 1864. From the 9th to the 13th, it was held by Federals and used as a base for raids on Lake City and Gainesville. On February 20 the site was used by Federals attacking Olustee. In the retreat from Olustee the camp again fell into Confederate hands.

—— Clay County ——

Green Cove Springs

MAGNOLIA SPRINGS CEMETERY
Haven Avenue

In 1864, Union forces established a strongpoint at Magnolia, a small community on the west bank of the St. Johns River, and used it as a base for conducting raids into the surrounding countryside. This cemetery contains the remains of at least 10 Union soldiers, including casualties from an October 1864 skirmish following a raid on Middleburg. In 2011, a 6-foot tall obelisk monument honoring Civil War soldiers was dedicated at the cemetery.

Middleburg

In October 1864, a small Union force of 55 men of the 4th Massachusetts Cavalry conducted a raid on Middleburg from their strongpoint at Magnolia near Green Cove Springs. The raiders burned warehouses and other buildings, and looted the remaining houses and businesses. Captain J.J. Dickison, commander of Confederate forces in the area, was notified of the raid and rushed to intercept them on their return to Magnolia. Near Halsey's Plantation, the Confederate force engaged the Union raiding party and routed them with heavy casualties in a skirmish known as the "Battle of Big Gum Creek." The Union forces reported losses of 29 killed, wounded and captured, while the Confederate report claimed slightly higher Union casualties of 33 to 35. The Confederate report stated that they had suffered no casualties but only lost several horses.

CLARK-CHALKER HOUSE
3891 Main Street

Signage in front of this house notes that it is the oldest extant residence in Clay County. Built in c.1835 for U.S. Army Captain Michael Clark, the house was purchased in 1859 by William S. Bardin, who served as a sergeant with the Confederate 1st Florida Reserves during the Civil War. His son, George N. Bardin, is reported to have served in a Home Guard unit. The Clark-Chalker House was looted during the October 1864 Union raid on Middleburg but was not burned as many other buildings were. The house was the post-war home of Albert S. Chalker, who married Bardin's daughter in December 1865. During the Civil War, Chalker served in the 2nd Florida Cavalry under Captain J.J. Dickison, and at one point in the war served under Brigadier General Joseph Finegan as a courier between Middle Florida and the mouth of the St. Johns River. The house is privately owned and is not open for tours.

—— Duval County ——

Jacksonville

By the time of the Civil War, Jacksonville was an important port city which dominated the St. Johns River route into the interior of East Florida. It was also the eastern terminus of the Florida, Atlantic & Gulf Central Railroad which ran to Lake City, and was a center for commercial lumbering mills. As such, it quickly became a focus for Union military activities and was occupied on four separate occasions. The first Union occupation occurred in March 1862, but the forces withdrew the following month. The second occupation by Union troops lasted four days in October 1862 and a third occupation lasted for 19 days in March 1863. The final Union occupation began in February 1864, when Jacksonville was seized for use as the base for a major expedition into Florida which culminated in the Battle of Olustee. After their defeat, the Union forces retreated back to Jacksonville where they fortified the city and remained until the end of the war in 1865. During this final occupation, Jacksonville was used as a base for conducting numerous Union raids along the St. Johns River and into East Florida.

Union Signal Tower at Jacksonville, 1864.
(Image courtesy of the State Archives of Florida)

Camp Milton Historic Preserve
1175 Halsema Road South
904.630.3516
www.campmilton.com

Designed and constructed in early 1864 at the direction of Confederate General Pierre G. T. Beauregard after the Battle of Olustee, Camp Milton served as the eastern headquarters for Confederate forces in Florida. With the construction of three miles of earthen and wood breastworks along the west bank of McGirts Creek, Beauregard planned this bastion to prevent Union advances from Jacksonville to the west toward the Confederate supply center and railhead at Baldwin. This camp, named for Florida's Civil War Governor John Milton, housed as many as 6,000 Confederate infantry and 1,500 cavalry troops in early 1864, but many of them were soon transferred to other theaters of the war. Several skirmishes were fought in the vicinity of Camp Milton and, in June 1864, a Union force from Jacksonville of some 2,500 men temporarily occupied Camp Milton after the outnumbered Confederate troops had withdrawn. After destroying much of the camp, the Union force withdrew back to Jacksonville, and Camp Milton was again occupied by Confederate troops. Camp Milton has been described as "one of the most significant [preserved earthworks] sites associated with the Civil War in Florida." Managed by the City of Jacksonville, the Camp Milton Historic Preserve provides educational programming through the site's Learning Center, which displays Civil War artifacts found on and around Camp Milton. Numerous interpretive panels throughout the site explain its history. The Road to Olustee Living History Weekend is an annual event held at the site in advance of the annual February Olustee Battle Reenactment.

Confederate artillery battery on St. Johns Bluff, 1862. *(Image courtesy of the State Archives of Florida)*

St. Johns Bluff

In early September 1862, Confederate Brigadier General Joseph Finegan ordered the construction of an artillery battery at St. Johns Bluff, downriver from Jacksonville. The Federals quickly learned of the Confederate presence and their gunboats engaged in several artillery duels with the Confederate defenders. On September 30, four Union transports left their base in South Carolina for the St. Johns River with about 1,500 troops. Union gunboats moved upriver in support of the land forces, which were to attack the Confederate positions from the rear. The advance of this powerful force unnerved the Confederate defenders. Lieutenant Colonel Charles Hopkins, commander at St. Johns Bluff, held a meeting with his officers and then ordered the abandonment of the position. During the hasty withdrawal the Confederates abandoned much equipment, including the bluff's artillery and ammunition.

In the aftermath, Federal forces occupied Jacksonville for a short period. It also opened the St. Johns River to incursions by Union gunboats. A court of inquiry exonerated Hopkins, stating that the force at his disposal had been inadequate to defend the position. Still, the events reflected no credit on the Confederacy, and opened northeast Florida to future Union occupations.

To learn more, see: "Military Operations on the St. Johns, September-October 1862 (Parts I & II)" by Edwin C. Bearss, *The Florida Historical Quarterly*, Vol. 42, Nos. 3 & 4, January & April 1964.

Confederate Monument, Jacksonville.
(Image courtesy of William Lees, Florida Public Archaeology Network)

Confederate Monument
117 West Duval Street

Located in Hemming Plaza, the monument was erected in 1898 and paid for by Charles C. Hemming, a wealthy banker and Confederate veteran. Hemming had joined the Jacksonville Light Infantry in 1861, fought in the western theater, and was captured at the Battle of Missionary Ridge in 1863. He escaped to Canada from where he participated in spying expeditions on Union fortifications in the Midwest, and eventually returned to the 3rd Florida Infantry in North Carolina where he ended the war as a sergeant-major. To honor Hemming for his donation, the City of Jacksonville changed the name of the monument site from St. James Park to Hemming Park in 1899.

NORTHEAST REGION

EVERGREEN CEMETERY
4535 Main Street
904.353.3649
www.evergreenjax.com

This cemetery contains the remains of over 250 Civil War veterans, both Confederate and Union. Among the notable Floridians are Captain John J. Dickison of the 2nd Florida Cavalry, who was known as the "Swamp Fox of the Confederacy" for his skill in defending the interior of Florida from Union raids and attacks; Lieutenant Colonel William Baya, who commanded the 8th Florida Infantry at the Battle of Gettysburg; James M. Baker, who served as a Senator from Florida in the Confederate Congress from 1862 to 1865 and for whom Baker County is named; Dr. Abel S. Baldwin, the chief surgeon for the Confederate Military District of East

Florida and for whom the Town of Baldwin in Duval County is named; Union Captain John F. Bartholf, an officer with the 2nd U.S. Colored Infantry during their Florida service; and Ossian B. Hart, a prominent Unionist who openly opposed Florida's secession and was Governor of Florida from 1873 to 1874. About 1905, the United Confederate Veterans erected a granite marker in the cemetery in honor of Dickison. Also in the cemetery, and very unusual for a Southern cemetery, is a large sculptured monument of a Civil War Union soldier erected in 1891 by the Grand Army of the Republic, a Union veteran's organization.

JACKSONVILLE HISTORICAL SOCIETY ARCHIVES
Jacksonville University
2800 University Boulevard North
904.256.7271
www.jaxhistory.com

Incorporated in 1929, the Jacksonville Historical Society's purpose is to foster and promote appreciation of the history of Jacksonville and northeast Florida. To this end, the society promotes the collection, preservation and presentation of materials pertaining to the area's history. The society maintains archives at the Swisher Library of Jacksonville University, with a collection that includes letters, diaries, and photographs related to the Civil War, as well as historical minutes of the Mary Martha Reid Chapter of the United Daughters of the Confederacy, Florida's first UDC Chapter. Access to the collection is by appointment.

MANDARIN MUSEUM AND HISTORICAL SOCIETY
11964 Mandarin Road
904.268.0784
www.mandarinmuseum.net
www.mapleleafshipwreck.com

The mission of the Mandarin Museum & Historical Society is to preserve buildings, artifacts and sites related to the history of Mandarin and its residents. A highlight of the collection

is the *Maple Leaf* exhibit. Leased to the Union Army by private investors, this 181-foot side-wheel paddle steamer served the Union occupiers of Jacksonville as a transport vessel on the St. Johns River. It was during one such trip on April 1, 1864, after delivering men and horses to Palatka, that the vessel blew up and sunk off Mandarin Point, the victim of a Confederate mine. Many years of archaeological work has yielded numerous artifacts which serve to depict the everyday life of Civil War soldiers. Exhibits include artifacts from the *Maple Leaf,* a scale model of the vessel, video of the salvage operations, and other Civil War objects. Edwin C. Bearss, Chief Historian Emeritus of the National Park Service, described this wreck as "unsurpassed as a source for Civil War material culture" and "the most important repository of Civil War artifacts ever found and probably will remain so." The Mandarin Museum is located at the Walter Jones Historical Park, a site that represents a typical 1800s Mandarin household and features a restored 1875 farmhouse and an 1876 barn.

Union Soldier Monument, Evergreen Cemetery, Jacksonville.
(Image courtesy of William Lees, Florida Public Archaeology Network)

Maple Leaf exhibit, Mandarin Museum, Jacksonville.
(Image courtesy of Sarah Miller, Florida Public Archaeology Network)

Mary Martha Reid.
(Image courtesy of the State Archives of Florida)

Mary Martha Reid

Mary Martha Reid became known during the Civil War for her work as matron of the Florida Hospital in Richmond. Soon after the outbreak of the war, Reid's son was serving in a Florida regiment in Virginia. While his presence undoubtedly contributed to Reid's decision to assist in the establishment of a hospital for the Florida troops in Virginia, the need for such a facility had become evident as the large number of sick and wounded flooded the Confederate capital during the first year of the war. Floridians donated money and material to supply the hospital, and the state provided additional funding. During its first year, it treated more than 1,000 patients and maintained a remarkably low death rate.

Confederate officials closed the Florida Hospital in December 1863. Reid subsequently worked at Howard's Grove Hospital near Richmond. In 1864, her son fell mortally wounded at the Battle of the Wilderness, and the grieving mother supervised his burial. Reid continued her work until the end of the war, fleeing the capital on the same train that carried President Jefferson Davis from the city. In recognition of her work, the Florida legislature passed an act in 1866 granting her $600 annually. She died in Fernandina in 1894.

To learn more, see: "Mary Martha Reid (1812-1894)" by David J. Coles, in *Women in the American Civil War,* edited by Lisa Tendrich Frank, ABC-CLIO, Inc., 2008.

Monument to the Women of the Confederacy, Jacksonville.
(Image courtesy of William Lees, Florida Public Archaeology Network)

MONUMENT TO THE WOMEN OF THE CONFEDERACY
956 Hubbard Street

It was during a 1900 Florida reunion of the United Confederate Veterans (UCV) that serious discussion of the possibility of a memorial to the Women of the Confederacy developed, and in 1901 the Florida Division of the UCV formally resolved to build such a monument. Dignan Park in the City of Jacksonville was selected as the monument site and UCV members raised $12,000, almost half the purchase price, with the Florida legislature providing the balance. The project got underway with the contracting of one of the nation's leading sculptors, Allen Newman. Construction on the 45-foot high rotunda began in July 1912. The installation of Newman's sculptures took place in mid-1915, and the formal dedication occurred in October 1915. Also in the park is a historical marker erected by the Sons of Confederate Veterans commemorating the May 1914 national reunion of Confederate veterans which drew an estimated 70,000 visitors to Jacksonville, including 8,000 veterans, many of whom camped in tents in Dignan Park. To commemorate the event, the City of Jacksonville changed the park name to Confederate Park in October 1914.

MUSEUM OF SCIENCE AND HISTORY
1025 Museum Circle
904.396.7062
www.themosh.org
www.mapleleafshipwreck.com

The Museum of Science and History strives to increase the knowledge and understanding of the natural environment and history of Jacksonville as well as northeast Florida. An exhibit on the Union transport *Maple Leaf* features an informational video/slide show, artifacts recovered from the vessel's wreckage, and an accurate scale model of the ship. The explosion of a Confederate torpedo (as underwater mines were referred to at the time) sank this 181-foot paddle-wheel vessel in the St. Johns River at Mandarin Point on April 1, 1864. Archaeological work began on the *Maple Leaf* in 1988. More than 3,000 individual artifacts have been recovered since that time. A State Historical Marker for the "Sinking of the *Maple Leaf*" is located across the St. Johns River from the museum at the Northbank Riverwalk.

MUSEUM OF SOUTHERN HISTORY
4304 Herschel Street
904.388.3574
www.museumsouthernhistory.com

This museum, established in 1975 by the Kirby Smith Camp 1209, Sons of Confederate Veterans, displays and interprets artifacts relating to the Civil War era. Visitors will find exhibits on military and civilian life during the Civil War. A 6,000 volume research library includes both period and later publications on the subject of the American Civil War.

OLD CITY CEMETERY
East Union Street between Washington & Cemetery Streets
www.metrojacksonville.com/article/2007-apr-a-walk-through-history-old-city-cemetery

This cemetery contains the remains of approximately 220 Confederate veterans, including Brigadier General Joseph Finegan who commanded Confederate forces at the Battle of Olustee and later commanded the Florida Brigade in

Old City Cemetery, Jacksonville.
(Image courtesy of William Lees, Florida Public Archaeology Network)

the Army of Northern Virginia; and Captain Francis P. Fleming of the 2nd Florida Infantry and 1st Florida Cavalry who commanded a volunteer company at the Battle of Natural Bridge and was governor of Florida from 1889 to 1893. One section of the Confederate plot contains the remains of those who resided at the Jacksonville Old Confederate Soldiers and Sailors Home, and contains a historical marker with information about the home erected by the Sons of Confederate Veterans. The Jacksonville home for aged and disabled Confederate veterans was in operation between 1893 and 1938, when the last veteran died.

SAMMIS PLANTATION HISTORICAL MARKER

200 Garrison Avenue

Erected by Old Arlington, Inc., this marker is located a short distance from the c.1850 Sammis House. The house was the residence of John S. Sammis, a prominent Unionist who, in 1862, was forced to flee Jacksonville until February 1864 when Union forces occupied the city for the fourth and final time. In 1863, Sammis was appointed a member of the Direct Tax Commission for Florida and took up his post in Fernandina. The Commission was created to implement the Direct Tax Law for the assessment and taxing of all real properties in areas under Federal control and, in some instances, the sale of abandoned property owned by Florida rebels for nonpayment of taxes. In April 1864, Sammis was one of the Florida delegates to the Republican Convention in Baltimore which renominated Abraham Lincoln for President. The house is privately owned and is not open for tours.

YELLOW BLUFF FORT HISTORIC STATE PARK

New Berlin Road
904.251.2320
www.floridastateparks.org/yellowbluff

Construction of a Confederate fortification at this site began in the summer of 1862 as part of General Robert E. Lee's coastal defense network for the Confederacy. The Yellow Bluff fort served a key role in defending Jacksonville from Union forces, as did the fortification at St. Johns Bluff across the St. Johns River (near present-day Fort Caroline National Memorial). The fortifications at Yellow Bluff consisted of earthworks and an artillery battery.

In October 1862, a major Federal expedition against Jacksonville of more than 1,500 soldiers, backed by several gunboats, resulted in Union troops occupying both Yellow Bluff and St. Johns Bluff, after the forced evacuation of the sites by the outnumbered Confederates. (See the "St. Johns Bluff" sidebar for more information.) As the Union troops evacuated Jacksonville after several days, and then returned again in 1863 and 1864, the Yellow Bluff fort changed hands several times. During the final Union occupation of Jacksonville beginning in February 1864, and lasting until the end of the war, a signal tower was erected by the U.S. Army Signal Corps at the Yellow Bluff fort and various regiments of U.S. Colored Troops prepared the site against possible Confederate attack. A commemorative monument to the Confederate defenders of Jacksonville, erected by the United Daughters of the Confederacy in 1950, is located at the site.

Civil War earthworks at Yellow Bluff Fort, Jacksonville.
(Image courtesy of William Lees, Florida Public Archaeology Network)

—— Nassau County ——

Fernandina Beach

By the time of the Civil War, Fernandina (the word Beach was added to the city's name in 1947) on Amelia Island was Florida's principal east coast port with a deep-water harbor and the eastern terminus of the Florida Railroad which ran across the state to Cedar Key. In March 1862, a Union fleet of some 26 vessels under the command of Navy Flag Officer Samuel F. DuPont arrived at Fernandina from its base at Port Royal, South Carolina. Confederate troops had been withdrawn in the face of this overwhelming Union force and both Fernandina and nearby Fort Clinch were captured without violence. Most of the community's residents also fled the island for Confederate held areas in the interior. For the remainder of the war, Fernandina was a center of operations for the Union navy's South Atlantic Blockading Squadron, a rest center for Union troops, and a base for Union raiding expeditions into the adjacent areas of Florida and Georgia. Various Union regiments and detachments of troops were stationed on Amelia Island through the course of the war, and occupied abandoned homes and other buildings in Fernandina. Fernandina also became a haven for Unionist refugees and escaped slaves from Florida and Georgia.

Union boat attacked by Confederate snipers near Fernandina. *(Image courtesy of the State Archives of Florida)*

AMELIA ISLAND LIGHTHOUSE
215½ Lighthouse Circle
904.277.7350
www.fbfl.us/index.aspx?NID=474

Constructed in 1839 using materials taken from the former 1820 Cumberland Island Lighthouse in Georgia, the Amelia Island Lighthouse is the oldest existing lighthouse in Florida. In June 1861, Confederate authorities ordered the lighthouse to be darkened and its lighting apparatus removed. The lens and other lighthouse equipment was shipped in November 1861 on the Florida Railroad to Waldo for safekeeping and then, in October 1864, moved to Madison. After the Union occupation of Amelia Island in March 1862, Federal military authorities recommended that the lighthouse be relit and, in 1864, the lighthouse was again operational. In 2001, the lighthouse was transferred

from the U.S. Coast Guard to the City of Fernandina Beach, which offers public tours of the site.

AMELIA ISLAND MUSEUM OF HISTORY
233 South 3rd Street
904.261.7378
www.ameliamuseum.org

Founded in 1975, the Amelia Island Museum of History is located in the restored 1938 Old County Jail building. The museum contains exhibits on the history of Nassau County including a dual exhibit that examines the Civil War on Amelia Island, as well as the impact on Florida of David Levy Yulee and his Florida Railroad. The Jaccard Research Library, a repository of images, letters, maps and other documents relating to Nassau County history, is available for research purposes.

Confederate Brigadier General Joseph Finegan.
(Image courtesy of the State Archives of Florida)

Joseph Finegan

Joseph Finegan was one of six Irish-born generals in the Confederate Army. Little is known of his early life, or when he arrived in America, though he eventually settled in Fernandina, partnering with David Yulee in the operation of the Florida Railroad, which linked Fernandina with Cedar Key. Finegan attended the Secession Convention and, when the war began, commanded the Fernandina Volunteers.

In April 1862, Finegan was promoted to brigadier general, and assumed command of the District of Middle and East Florida. Later the district was divided, with Finegan exercising authority over the area east of the Suwannee River. Early in February 1864, Federal forces mounted their largest invasion of Florida. To meet this threat, Finegan consolidated his scattered troops and, with reinforcements from Georgia, constructed entrenchments near Olustee, east of Lake City. The ensuing Battle of Olustee on February 20

resulted in a resounding Confederate victory with the Union force retreating back to Jacksonville.

In May 1864, Finegan took reinforcements to Virginia and assumed command of the Army of Northern Virginia's Florida Brigade. In March 1865, suffering from exhaustion, he resigned and returned to Florida. After the war, Finegan spent one term in the Florida legislature, and then moved to Savannah before returning to Florida, where he died in 1885.

To learn more, see: "Joseph Finegan: Fernandina's Confederate General" by Charles Litrico, *Amelia Now*, Fall 1998. (Also available online at: www.amelianow.com/fall98finegan.htm)

BOSQUE BELLO CEMETERY
1320 North 14th Street

This cemetery contains the remains of both Confederate and Union Civil War veterans, including Confederate navy Lieutenant Edward J.K. Johnston, who died of illness while in a Union prisoner of war (POW) camp at Fort Warren, Massachusetts in 1863. Due to post closings, the Federal government moved his grave three times in New England with his last resting place at Fort Devens, Massachusetts. In 2002, he was reinterred in the Bosque Bello Cemetery in his hometown. It is believed that Lieutenant Johnston was the last Confederate POW buried in New England to be returned to the South.

FIRST PRESBYTERIAN CHURCH
19 North 6th Street
904.261.3837
www.1stpres-fb.com/history.htm

Constructed in 1859, this church was used as a military barracks for Union troops during the Federal occupation of Fernandina and later as a primary school operated by the Freedmen's Bureau for teaching freed slaves. It is reported that Union troops planned to confiscate the church bell to melt it down for armaments, but that a Union officer, Major W.B.C. Duryee, intervened and prevented its dismantling.

FLORIDA HOUSE INN
22 South 3rd Street
904.491.3322 or toll-free 1.800.258.3301
www.floridahouseinn.com

Constructed in 1857 by the Florida Railroad Company, it is among the state's oldest surviving tourist hotels. During the Federal occupation of Fernandina, the house was occupied by Union troops for officers quarters. The house is now operated as a bed and breakfast inn.

The Peninsula Newspaper printed in Union-occupied Fernandina, 1864.
(Image courtesy of the State Archives of Florida)

FORT CLINCH STATE PARK
2601 Atlantic Avenue
904.277.7274
www.floridastateparks.org/fortclinch

Construction of Fort Clinch began in 1847, and today it is considered one of the best preserved 19th century forts in the nation. Sited on the northern tip of Amelia Island, this fort provided protection for the deep-water port of Fernandina. In January 1861, as Florida prepared to secede from the Union, Florida militia seized Fort Clinch from its lone Federal fort keeper and two laborers. While under Confederate control, additional cannons from Fort Marion in St. Augustine were sent to

Fort Clinch and the fort served as a safe haven for blockade runners. In late 1861, General Robert E. Lee, then commanding the Department of South Carolina, Georgia and Florida, personally inspected Confederate defenses on Amelia Island, and in February 1862 authorized their evacuation because of the Union's superior naval forces. The withdrawal had not been completed when, in March 1862, a large Union invasion flotilla approached Amelia Island and forced a hasty evacuation of Fort Clinch by the remaining Confederate troops. Union forces occupied the fort from that point until the end of the Civil War, and at least 14 different Union regiments were stationed there during the war. Fort Clinch was declared surplus government property and sold to local Fernandina developers in 1926. In 1935, the property was purchased by the State of Florida. Visitor center exhibits tell the fort's history, and Fort Clinch park staff and volunteers in Civil War uniforms provide living history programming on a daily basis. Larger reenactments occur on the first full weekend of each month during the "First Weekend Union Garrisons", and also during "Confederate Garrison" events.

Fort Clinch, Fernandina Beach. *(Image courtesy of William Lees, Florida Public Archaeology Network)*

MERRICK-SIMMONS HOUSE
102 South 10th Street

After the Union occupation of Fernandina in 1862, this c.1860 house was used as a hospital for Union troops. In June 1863, the property passed to the ownership of Chloe Merrick in a tax sale of abandoned Confederate properties and she owned it until 1865. Merrick had arrived in Fernandina from Syracuse, New York in late 1862 as the agent for the National Freedman's Relief Association of New York, and had helped establish a Freedman's School in Fernandina's Episcopal Church, where she taught freed slaves. In 1863, she also established and organized the Fernandina orphanage in the abandoned home of Confederate Brigadier General Joseph Finegan, which was also purchased in a tax sale. After the war, Merrick married Harrison Reed, who was Governor of Florida from 1869 to 1873. A Great Floridian 2000 plaque for Chloe Merrick is located on this house. The house was most recently used for commercial offices and is not open for tours.

WILLIAMS HOUSE
103 South 9th Street
904.277.2328 or toll-free 1.800.414.9258
www.williamshouse.com

Confederate President Jefferson Davis was a friend of the Williams family and was a guest in this c.1856 house. It is reported that some of his personal effects were stored in the Williams House during the Civil War. After the Federal occupation of the city in 1862, the Williams family fled to Waldo, and the house was used by Union troops as officers quarters. The adjacent c.1859 Hearthstone building on the Williams House property was used as an infirmary for Union troops. The house is now operated as a bed and breakfast inn.

Confederate Monument, Palatka.
(Image courtesy of William Lees, Florida Public Archaeology Network)

Putnam County

Palatka

During the Civil War, several Confederate military camps were located in the Palatka area, including a number in the vicinity of present-day Ravine Gardens State Park. However, after Union gunboats gained control of the St. Johns River in 1862, most residents of Palatka abandoned the city and resettled in nearby Orange Springs and Florahome. Throughout 1862, while raiding plantations along the St. Johns River, Union gunboats periodically landed at Palatka, which they found mostly deserted. However, in March 1863, an attempted landing at Palatka by Union soldiers from two regiments of U.S.

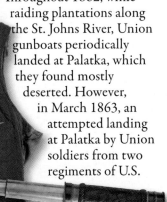

Union army officer's vest and Civil War-era telescope.
(Images courtesy of the Museum of Florida History)

Colored Troops was repulsed by the 2nd Florida Cavalry under the command of Captain J.J. Dickison. Dickison reported that the Union force had suffered 20 to 30 casualties of dead and wounded while the Confederates suffered one man wounded. In March 1864, a strong Union force commanded by Colonel William Barton occupied Palatka where they moved into deserted buildings and erected earthworks surrounding the town. Several skirmishes were fought between Union pickets and Confederate forces around Palatka until April 1864 when the Federal force evacuated the city. In July 1864, Palatka was again occupied by a strong Union force which skirmished with Confederate troops until August 1864, when the Federal troops abandoned Palatka for the duration of the war. In 1924, a Confederate monument was erected in Palatka by the United Daughters of the Confederacy on the Putnam County Courthouse lawn.

BRONSON-MULHOLLAND HOUSE
100 Madison Street
386.329.0140
www.rootsweb.ancestry.com/~flpchs/virtual_tour.htm

The Bronson-Mulholland House was constructed in 1854 by United States District Judge Isaac Bronson. After his death in 1855, his widow Sophronia Bronson remained at the house until the outbreak of the Civil War when she returned to her former home in New York. During the war, the vacant house was occupied by Confederate soldiers and, during the Federal occupations of Palatka, used as quarters by Union troops. After the war, in 1866, a Freedman's School, supported by the New York branch of the Freedmen's Union Commission for teaching freed slaves, was opened in the house by Charlotte J. Henry, a friend of Sophronia Bronson. Acquired by the City of Palatka in 1965, the house is operated by the Putnam County Historical Society as a museum of local history.

FORT SHANNON OFFICERS QUARTERS

110 Madison Street
386.329.0140

Believed to have been constructed in c.1842 as a part of the Seminole War era Fort Shannon, the building was in private ownership by the time of the Civil War. It was used as a military barracks by Union troops during their occupations of Palatka. Originally located at 224 North 1st Street, the building was relocated to its current site adjacent to the Bronson-Mulholland House in 1984 as part of the Putnam County Historical Society's historic museum complex. Operated by the Society as the Putnam Historic Museum, this building contains exhibit cases of Civil War period objects.

ST. MARK'S EPISCOPAL CHURCH

200 North Main Street
386.328.1474
http://stmarkspalatka.net/history.aspx

Constructed in 1854, this is the oldest church in Palatka. During the Federal occupations of Palatka, the church was used as a military barracks for Union troops. A State Historical Marker at the site provides information on the church's history.

WESTVIEW CEMETERY

Crill Avenue and Osceola Street

This cemetery contains the remains of at least 49 Confederate veterans, including Captain Winston J.T. Stephens of the 2nd Florida Cavalry who was killed during a skirmish at Cedar Creek west of Jacksonville in 1864, and Colonel Hubbard L. Hart, an assistant quartermaster and the owner of two steamboats which were used by the Confederacy to transport supplies. Also buried here is James O. Devall, a delegate to the Florida Secession Convention and the owner of the *General Sumpter,* the first steamboat built in Palatka. In March 1864, the *General Sumpter* was captured by the Union gunboat USS *Columbine* in Lake George south of Palatka with all its officers and crew. The cemetery also contains the remains of at least 20 Union veterans including at least 11 soldiers of the U.S. Colored Troops.

Skirmish at Braddock's Farm near Welaka in 1865, from *Dickison and His Men.*
(Image courtesy of the State Archives of Florida)

Unionism

While most Floridians supported secession in 1860-1861, a number still exhibited a lingering loyalty to the United States. As the war progressed, anti-war and pro-Union sentiment in the state increased. Some may have originally opposed secession, while others became demoralized and disenchanted with Confederate policies. Conscription alienated many, as did the Impressment Act, which authorized the government's seizure of food and other goods. Widespread shortages and long casualty lists added to the discontent.

As anti-war and pro-Union sentiment increased, some Unionists fled to the protection of Federal military forces. Others hid in remote areas of the state, their numbers augmented by deserters who grew in number as the war progressed. In addition to the white population, large numbers of Florida slaves, with no loyalty to the Confederacy, likewise fled to the protection of Union forces.

The strongest example of militant Unionism in Florida was the formation of the 1st and 2nd Florida Union Cavalry Regiments, which served in the Federal army. These units took part in numerous skirmishes during 1864-1865. Though not all Florida Unionists demonstrated their opposition to the Confederacy to that extent, it appears obvious that, while many Floridians

Lieutenant Frederick Jost, 1st Florida Union Cavalry.
(Image courtesy of the Museum of Florida History)

remained loyal to their new nation until the final surrender, others had long since abandoned the cause and looked to the Union victory with satisfaction or relief.

To learn more, see: "Deprivation, Disaffection, and Desertion in Confederate Florida" by John F. Reiger, *The Florida Historical Quarterly*, Vol. 48, No. 3, January 1970.

—— St. Johns County ——

St. Augustine

Founded by the Spanish in 1565, St. Augustine is the nation's oldest continuously occupied European city and port. Between 1672 and 1695, the Spanish constructed a massive coquina fort at St. Augustine, the Castillo de San Marcos, which was renamed Fort Marion by the Americans after Spain ceded Florida to the United States in 1821. On the eve of Florida's withdrawal from the Union in early January 1861, under orders from Governor Madison S. Perry, state militia seized the fort without violence. During the first year of the Civil War, several Confederate blockade runners operated out of the port of St. Augustine. Confederate forces occupied St. Augustine until March 1862 when they withdrew from the city to prevent civilian casualties as Union warships approached. Many of the city's residents also fled to Confederate held areas in the state's interior. Union forces occupied St. Augustine, and strengthened the defenses at Fort Marion and other areas around the city. For the duration of the war, St. Augustine was under Union control and was used mainly as a rest center for Union troops. St. Augustine also became a haven for Unionist refugees and escaped slaves. Nearly 150 local African Americans were recruited for service in the 21st, 33rd, and 34th U.S. Colored Infantry regiments. Although the Confederates never directly attacked the garrison at Fort Marion, Confederate forces under the command of Captain J.J. Dickison occasionally skirmished on the outskirts of the city with Union troops sent out to gather firewood. One such skirmish in March 1863 resulted in the capture of five Union soldiers. A second and larger skirmish in December 1863 resulted in six Union soldiers killed or wounded and 24 taken prisoner, while the Confederates reported no casualties.

ARRIVAS HOUSE

46 St. George Street
904.825.5033
http://staugustinegovernment.com/your_government/PurposeofHT.cfm

Constructed in c.1740, this house was the residence of Paul Arnau, the St. Augustine Collector of Customs and Superintendent of Lighthouses. In January 1861, Confederate authorities ordered the St. Augustine Lighthouse to be darkened. Arnau oversaw its darkening, and the later removal of its lighting apparatus. Arnau also ordered that the lighting apparatus at the Cape Canaveral Lighthouse be removed, and is believed to have organized the group that, in August 1861, removed the lenses and machinery from the Jupiter Inlet Lighthouse and wrecked the lighting mechanism on the Cape Florida Lighthouse. Elected mayor of St. Augustine in November 1861, Arnau resigned that post in March 1862 rather than surrender the city to the Union navy. After the Union occupation of the city, Arnau was arrested and taken aboard the USS *Isaac Smith*. He was released after lighting mechanisms from the St. Augustine and Cape Canaveral Lighthouses, as well as other lighthouse equipment which he had stored at his house, were returned to the Union navy.

DUMMETT HOUSE (ST. FRANCIS INN)

279 St. George Street
904.824.6068 or toll-free 1.800.824.6062
www.stfrancisinn.com

Owned by Confederate Lieutenant General William J. Hardee, this c.1791 house was the residence of his sister-in-law Anna Dummett, an ardent Confederate

Edmund Kirby Smith

The highest ranking Floridian in Confederate military service was Edmund Kirby Smith. Born in St. Augustine in 1824, he graduated from West Point and fought in the Mexican War. In 1861, Smith resigned his commission and joined the Confederate army. Quickly rising to the rank of brigadier general, Smith was wounded at the First Battle of Bull Run (Manassas). In the fall of 1861, he earned promotion to major general and the following spring was put in command of East Tennessee and took part in the invasion of Kentucky. Despite a relatively undistinguished career to this point, Smith was promoted to lieutenant general and placed in command of the vast Department of the Trans-Mississippi, the region west of the Mississippi River. He was criticized by some for inaction during the Vicksburg campaign, and for overemphasizing operations in Arkansas and Missouri at the expense of Louisiana. Nonetheless, President Davis promoted Smith to full general and, as the war progressed, he maintained such autonomy that the region became known as "Kirby Smithdom." He went into exile in Mexico at the war's end before returning to the United States. When Smith died in 1893, he was the last surviving full general of the Confederacy.

To learn more, see: *General Edmund Kirby Smith, C.S.A.* by Joseph H. Parks, Louisiana State University Press, 1954, reprint 1982 Southern Biography Series.

Confederate General Edmund Kirby Smith.
(Image courtesy of the Library of Congress)

Fort Marion, Castillo de San Marcos National Monument, St. Augustine. *(Image courtesy of William Lees, Florida Public Archaeology Network)*

supporter, who raised the widowed Hardee's four children there while he served as Commandant of Cadets at West Point and then later as a Confederate corps commander in the western theater. In 1864, Hardee was placed in command of the Military Department of South Carolina, Georgia, and Florida, where he opposed Sherman's March to the Sea. After the war, in 1866, Anna Dummett became the first president of the St. Augustine Ladies Memorial Association and led the effort to raise funds for the erection of the city's Confederate monument. The house is now operated as a bed and breakfast inn.

FORT MARION, CASTILLO DE SAN MARCOS NATIONAL MONUMENT

1 South Castillo Avenue
904.829.6506
www.nps.gov/casa

For protection of their interests in *La Florida,* the Spanish began construction of Castillo de San Marcos in 1672. Constructed of coquina quarried on nearby Anastasia Island, the fort is the only surviving 17th century military structure in the United States. After Spain ceded Florida to the United States in 1821, the Americans changed the name of the Castillo to Fort Marion in 1825. On the eve of the Civil War, the U.S. military presence had largely been withdrawn from St. Augustine and Fort Marion's caretaker garrison consisted of one ordnance sergeant. As the Secession Convention was meeting in Tallahassee in early January 1861, Governor Madison S. Perry ordered the seizure of Fort Marion. On January 7, 1861, state militia from St. Augustine and Fernandina seized the fort without violence. During the remainder of 1861, a number of artillery pieces were removed from Fort Marion to reinforce Confederate troops at Fort Clinch near Fernandina, the St. Johns Bluff, and outside the state. Confederate forces occupied Fort Marion until March 1862, when they evacuated St. Augustine. Union forces occupied the abandoned Fort Marion, strengthened its defenses, and remained at the fort for the duration of the war. No Confederate attempt was made to retake the fort. In 1933, Fort Marion was transferred from the War Department to the National Park Service, and, in 1942, the fort's name was restored to Castillo de San Marcos.

GOVERNMENT HOUSE

48 King Street
904.825.5079
www.staugustinegovernment.com/visitors/gov-house.cfm

On March 11, 1862, a small Union landing party under the command of Naval Commander C. R. P. Rogers proceeded to the Government House, the seat of local government constructed in the early 1700s. There, Commander Rogers informed the St. Augustine City Council of the terms of surrender for the city. After the Federal occupation of the city, the building was used as a military barracks, a hospital and a theater for Union troops. The building contains a museum with a Civil War exhibit containing period artifacts and historic photographs of St. Augustine.

LLAMBIAS HOUSE
31 St. Francis Street
904.825.2333
www.staugustinehistoricalsociety.org

Constructed in c.1763, this house was the residence of the Llambias family, whose three sons served in the St. Augustine Blues, 3rd Florida Infantry and whose father was briefly imprisoned in Fort Marion for refusing to take a loyalty oath after Union troops occupied St. Augustine. The Llambias family was eventually permitted through the Federal lines and settled in the Confederate-held area of the state until the end of the war. Returning after the war, they found the house had been stripped of its furniture and woodwork, and that the ground floor had been used as a stable by Union troops.

Loring Monument, St. Augustine.
(Image courtesy of William Lees, Florida Public Archaeology Network)

LORING MEMORIAL
48 King Street

This monument was erected in 1920 on the Government House grounds by the United Daughters of the Confederacy in honor of Confederate Major General William Wing Loring. Loring spent his childhood in St. Augustine, and his ashes are imbedded in the foundation of the monument.

MARKLAND (ANDERSON HOUSE)
102 King Street
904.829.6481
www.flagler.edu

Constructed in 1839-1842, this house was the residence of Dr. Andrew Anderson II who enlisted in the local Confederate military unit, the St. Augustine Blues, at the outbreak of the war. In early 1862, he paid for a substitute to take his place in the Blues unit (as allowed by Confederate policy) and left Florida to return to medical school at the College of Physicians and Surgeons in New York City. In 1864, he provided medical services to Union soldiers at Fredericksburg, Virginia field hospitals by treating those who were wounded during General Ulysses S. Grant's campaign that year. His mother, Clarissa Anderson, a staunch Unionist, remained at Markland during the war and tended to sick and wounded soldiers at the Union army hospital. This historic house is presently used for special events by Flagler College, as well as for faculty and staff offices. Special sponsored tours are occasionally available.

Llambias House (center left), St. Augustine, post Civil War.
(Image courtesy of Charles Tingley, St. Augustine Historical Society)

Hispanics

With its long history as a Spanish colony, it is not surprising that Florida maintained a vibrant Hispanic population at the time of the Civil War. Centered primarily in Pensacola and St. Augustine, with smaller numbers scattered throughout the peninsula, the Hispanic population of Civil War era Florida was descended from the colonists who had remained there following the American acquisition of the territory.

Most Southern Hispanics gave their support to the Confederacy following secession. One roster for the entire Confederacy lists more than 6,000 soldiers, sailors, and marines of Hispanic ancestry, along with civil officials, blockade runners, and even a few female spies. Of those listed in this roster, the great majority came from Texas and Louisiana, but Florida appears to rank third, with more than 300 Hispanics who served in Florida units or with some connection to the state. Every Florida Confederate military unit had at least one member with a Hispanic name on its roll, but the two Florida units with the largest number of Hispanics appear to have been the 3rd and the 8th Infantry Regiments. The Florida Independent Blues, later Company B of the 3rd Florida Infantry, was probably the most ethnically diverse unit from the state. Many of St. Augustine's established Hispanic families joined its ranks.

To learn more, see: "Ancient City Defenders: The St. Augustine Blues" by David J. Coles, *El Escribano*, Vol. 23, 1986.

PLAZA DE LA CONSTITUCION
Between Cathedral Place and King Street

Established in accordance with the Spanish Royal Ordinance of 1573 for town plans, the Plaza, or Public Square, in the center of the colonial city contains several monuments and historic objects, including:

Confederate Monument

Originally erected in 1872 on private property on St. George Street by the St. Augustine Ladies Memorial Association, the monument was rebuilt in the Plaza in 1879 reusing material from

the original monument. The names of 46 Confederate war dead from St. Augustine are listed on the monument.

Civil War Ordnance

Mounted in the Plaza are two Civil War 32-pounder rifled cannons and two Civil War 8-inch Columbiad cannons from Fort Marion. The cannons were presented to the city by the U.S. War Department in 1900. In the adjacent Anderson Circle, there is a Civil War seacoast mortar from Fort Marion also given to the city by the U.S. War Department at about the same time.

SAN LORENZO CEMETERY
1635 US Highway 1 South

This cemetery contains the remains of at least 93 Confederate soldiers and sailors including 3 black Confederate veterans who served as musicians in the 3rd Florida Infantry, as well as 7 black Union soldiers of the U.S. Colored Troops.

SEGUI-KIRBY SMITH HOUSE
12 Aviles Street
904.825.2333
www.staugustinehistoricalsociety.org/library.html

Constructed in the late 1700s by Bernardo Segui, this was the childhood home of Edmund Kirby Smith, a West Point graduate and the last Confederate general to surrender his command, who was born here in May 1824. In early 1863, Union authorities exiled the general's mother, Frances Kirby Smith, from the city for spying, and

she relocated to Madison. A research library, which includes Civil War period archives, is now maintained at this site by the St. Augustine Historical Society. The collection is open to the public for research and is composed of files and books on Florida history, including those on the Civil War period and the Kirby Smith family. There are two bronze statues in the garden of General Kirby Smith and a plaque inside commemorating its famous former resident.

ST. AUGUSTINE HISTORICAL SOCIETY
14 St. Francis Street
904.825.2333
www.staugustinehistoricalsociety.org

In addition to the Research Library at the Segui-Kirby Smith House, the Society operates the Oldest House Museum Complex, which includes the Manucy Museum in the 1924 Webb Building. This museum contains exhibits on local and regional history, including a Civil War exhibit with period artifacts.

ST. AUGUSTINE LIGHTHOUSE AND MUSEUM
81 Lighthouse Avenue
904.829.0745
www.staugustinelighthouse.com

The existing St. Augustine Lighthouse was constructed in 1874 to replace an earlier 1824 lighthouse which had stood during the Civil War and was threatened by erosion. Located about 500 yards northeast of the present lighthouse, it collapsed in 1880. A State Historical Marker for "Sentinels of the Coast" is located near its site. Exhibits in the restored 1876 Keeper's House tell the story of the original lighthouse and the port of St. Augustine during the Civil War. The Lighthouse Archaeological Maritime Program (LAMP), the research arm of the Lighthouse and Museum, conducts underwater archaeological work in St. Johns County waters. A current LAMP project involves the

search for the *Jefferson Davis,* a Confederate privateer which captured nine Northern merchant vessels off the coast of New England before wrecking on St. Augustine's inlet bar in August 1861.

ST. AUGUSTINE NATIONAL CEMETERY
104 Marine Street
352.793.7740
www.cem.va.gov/cems/nchp/staugustine.asp

This cemetery contains at least 33 Union troops and veterans, including Union sailors who died while on duty at Egmont Key and whose remains were relocated here in 1909 as part of the nationwide effort to consolidate military burials. The highest ranking Union officer interred here is Brigadier General Martin D. Hardin of Illinois, who served during the war in the Army of the Potomac and was a personal friend of President Abraham Lincoln. The cemetery also contains the remains of at least two Confederate veterans.

ST. FRANCIS BARRACKS
82 Marine Street
904.823.0364
www.floridaguard.army.mil

Originally constructed in the early to mid-1700s, this building was used as a military barracks first for Confederate troops, and then for Union troops after the Federal occupation of St. Augustine in 1862. Now the headquarters of the Florida National Guard, the Barracks contains a small museum on the military history of Florida, including the Civil War. The museum is open by appointment.

TOLOMATO CEMETERY
14 Cordova Street
www.tolomatocemetery.com

This cemetery contains the remains of Union veterans and at least 17 Confederate veterans. Also buried here is Florida Catholic Bishop Augustin Verot, known as the "Rebel Bishop" for his defense of the Confederate cause. After the Civil War, Bishop Verot became an advocate for the rights of freed slaves and oversaw the establishment of a school for their education in St. Augustine by the Sisters of St. Joseph.

Segui-Kirby Smith House, St. Augustine.
(Image courtesy of Charles Tingley, St. Augustine Historical Society)

NORTHWEST REGION
(PAGES 9-21)

Bay County
- Union Soldier Monument
- Confederate Salt Kettle
- St. Andrew Bay Saltworks State Historical Marker
- St. Andrew Skirmish State Historical Marker

Escambia County
- Barrancas National Cemetery
- Fort Barrancas
- Fort Pickens
- Historic Pensacola Village
- Hyer-Knowles Planing Mill
- Confederate Monument, Lee Square
- Pensacola Lighthouse
- Pensacola Navy Yard
- St. Johns Cemetery
- St. Michael's Cemetery

Franklin County
- Chestnut Street Cemetery
- Orman House Historic State Park
- Raney House
- Trinity Episcopal Church
- Cape St. George Lighthouse
- Fort Gadsden

Gulf County
- St. Joseph Saltworks State Historical Marker

Jackson County
- Battle of Marianna Historical Markers
- Confederate Monument
- Battle of Marianna Monument
- Davis-West House
- Ely-Criglar House Historical Marker
- Holden House Historical Marker
- Riverside Cemetery
- St. Luke's Cemetery

Liberty County
- Torreya State Park

Okaloosa County
- Fort Walton Beach Heritage Park & Cultural Center

Santa Rosa County
- Bagdad Cemetery
- Bagdad Village Museum & Complex
- Thompson House and Civil War Skirmish State Historical Marker
- Arcadia Mill Site

Walton County
- Confederate Monument

Washington County
- Moss Hill United Methodist Church

NORTH CENTRAL REGION
(PAGES 22-38)

Alachua County
- Cotton Wood Plantation State Historical Marker
- Battle of Gainesville State Historical Marker
- Confederate Monument
- Bailey House State Historical Marker
- Evergreen Cemetery
- Haile Homestead at Kanapaha Plantation
- Matheson Museum Complex
- Old Gainesville Depot
- P.K. Yonge Library of Florida History, University of Florida
- Oak Ridge Cemetery
- Dudley Farm Historic State Park
- J. J. Dickison and Davis Baggage Train State Historical Marker

Bradford County
- Captain Richard Bradford State Historical Marker

Columbia County
- Battle of Olustee Monument
- Lake City-Columbia County Historical Museum
- Oaklawn Cemetery

Gadsden County
- Chattahoochee Arsenal
- CSS Chattahoochee Monument
- Confederate Monument
- A.K. Allison House
- Smallwood-White House State Historical Marker
- Soldiers Cemetery in Eastern Cemetery
- The Quincy Academy State Historical Marker
- Western Cemetery

Hamilton County
- Riverside Cemetery

Jefferson County
- Lloyd Railroad Depot
- Confederate Monument
- Old City and Roseland Cemeteries
- Palmer Family Graveyard and Palmer-Perkins House

Leon County
- Bellevue (Murat House)
- Brokaw-McDougall House
- Florida Historic Capitol
- Confederate Monument
- Florida State University Libraries Special Collections and Archives, Strozier Library
- Fort Houstoun
- Jacksonville, Pensacola & Mobile Railroad Company Freight Depot
- Knott House Museum
- Meginnis-Munroe House
- Museum of Florida History
- Old City Cemetery
- State Archives of Florida/State Library of Florida
- St. Johns Episcopal Church Cemetery
- Tallahassee-St. Marks Historic Railroad State Trail
- The Grove
- Union Bank
- Natural Bridge Battlefield Historic State Park

Levy County
- Cedar Key Historical Society Museum
- Cedar Key Museum State Park
- Old Island Hotel
- Cedar Keys Lighthouse

Madison County
- Confederate Monument, Four Freedoms Park
- Oakland Cemetery
- Oak Ridge Cemetery
- Treasures of Madison County Museum and Madison County Genealogical Library
- Wardlaw-Smith-Goza House

Suwannee County
- Suwannee River State Park

Taylor County
- Taylor County Saltworks State Historical Marker

Wakulla County
- Wakulla History Museum & Archives
- Fort Ward, San Marcos de Apalache Historic State Park
- St. Marks Lighthouse

NORTHEAST REGION
(PAGES 39-53)

Baker County
- Olustee Battlefield Historic State Park
- Sanderson Camp State Historical Marker

Clay County
- Magnolia Springs Cemetery
- Clark-Chalker House

Duval County
- Camp Milton Historic Preserve
- Confederate Monument
- Evergreen Cemetery
- Jacksonville Historical Society Archives
- Mandarin Museum and Historical Society
- Monument to the Women of the Confederacy
- Museum of Science and History
- Museum of Southern History
- Old City Cemetery
- Sammis Plantation Historical Marker
- Yellow Bluff Fort Historic State Park

Nassau County
- Amelia Island Lighthouse
- Amelia Island Museum of History
- Bosque Bello Cemetery
- First Presbyterian Church
- Florida House Inn
- Fort Clinch State Park
- Merrick-Simmons House
- Williams House

Putnam County
- Confederate Monument
- Bronson-Mulholland House
- Fort Shannon Officers Quarters
- St. Mark's Episcopal Church
- Westview Cemetery

St. Johns County
- Arrivas House
- Dummett House (St. Francis Inn)
- Fort Marion, Castillo de San Marcos National Monument
- Government House
- Llambias House
- Loring Memorial
- Markland (Anderson House)
- Confederate Monument, Plaza de la Constitucion
- San Lorenzo Cemetery
- Segui-Kirby Smith House
- St. Augustine Historical Society
- St. Augustine Lighthouse and Museum
- St. Augustine National Cemetery
- St. Francis Barracks
- Tolomato Cemetery

CENTRAL REGION
(PAGES 56-58)

Marion County
- Confederate Monument
- Marshall Plantation State Historical Marker
- Silver River Museum & Environmental Education Center
- Orange Springs Community Church and Cemetery

Orange County
- Confederate Monument
- Greenwood Cemetery

Osceola County
- St. Cloud Heritage Museum

Polk County
- Oak Hill Cemetery
- Polk County Historical Museum
- Fort Meade Historical Museum
- Confederate Monument

Seminole County
- Geneva Cemetery

CENTRAL EAST REGION
(PAGE 59)

Brevard County
- The Florida Historical Society

Volusia County
- De Leon Springs State Park
- New Smyrna Museum of History
- Old Fort Park

CENTRAL WEST REGION
(PAGES 60-65)

Citrus County
- Yulee Sugar Mill Ruins Historic State Park
- The Old Courthouse Heritage Museum

Hernando County
- Confederate Monument
- May-Stringer House
- Bayport Park

Hillsborough County
- Egmont Key Lighthouse
- East Hillsborough Historical Society Museum
- Confederate Monument
- Fort Brooke Battery
- Oaklawn Cemetery
- Tampa Blockade Runners and Battle of Ballast Point Historical Markers
- Woodlawn Cemetery

Pinellas County
- Greenwood Cemetery
- Miranda Home State Historical Marker

SOUTHWEST REGION
(PAGES 66-69)

Hendry County
- Fort Thompson State Historical Marker

Lee County
- Fort Myers Attack State Historical Marker
- Monument to U. S. Colored Troops
- Southwest Florida Museum of History

Manatee County
- Confederate Monument
- Curry Settlement Homes
- First Manatee County Courthouse
- Manatee Burying Ground Cemetery
- Manatee County Historical Records Library
- South Florida Museum
- Gamble Plantation Historic State Park

SOUTHEAST REGION
(PAGES 70-76)

Miami-Dade County
- Cape Florida Lighthouse
- City of Miami Cemetery
- Union Monument

Monroe County
- Fort Jefferson
- Union Monuments
- East and West Martello Towers
- Fort Zachary Taylor Historic State Park
- Hemingway House
- Key West Cemetery
- Key West Lighthouse
- "Key West Oldest House"
- Mallory Homesite Historical Marker
- Naval Base Key West

Palm Beach County
- Jupiter Inlet Lighthouse
- Woodlawn Cemetery

55

— Marion County —

Ocala

CONFEDERATE MONUMENT
2601 SE Fort King Street

This monument was erected in 1908 by the United Daughters of the Confederacy beside the Marion County Courthouse in the downtown Ocala Public Square. Although a new larger county courthouse was constructed in 1965 and then expanded in 1991, the monument remained in front of the courthouse until 2007 when another expansion resulted in its relocation to a nook on the building's south side. In August 2010, it was moved to the Ocala-Marion County Veterans Memorial Park.

MARSHALL PLANTATION STATE HISTORICAL MARKER
**Sharpe's Ferry Road
at Ocklawaha River Bridge
East of Ocala**

A State Historical Marker for the "Marshall Plantation Site" is located a short distance south of the sugar plantation of Jehu Foster Marshall. From South Carolina, Marshall established his Florida plantation in 1855. At the outbreak of the war, Marshall returned to his native state to serve as

Unveiling of Confederate Monument at Ocala, 1908. *(Image courtesy of the State Archives of Florida)*

colonel in Orr's 1ˢᵗ South Carolina Rifles, and was killed at the Battle of Second Bull Run (Second Manassas) in August 1862. Under the supervision of his widow, the plantation continued to supply syrup and sugar to the Confederacy. In March 1865, an expedition of U.S. Colored Troops from Jacksonville moved south into

Marion County to raid area plantations. The Marshall Plantation and sugar mill were destroyed. The Ocala Home Guard militia attacked the raiding force as they were leaving the plantation, and a running skirmish was fought to the Ocklawaha River. The Union force withdrew across the river and set fire to the bridge, blocking

Captain J.J. Dickison, 2nd Florida Cavalry.
(Image courtesy of the State Archives of Florida)

John Jackson Dickison

The most prominent Confederate partisan leader in Florida, the legendary Captain J.J. Dickison helped maintain Confederate control over north-central Florida during the war's later years. When the war began, Dickison served in the Marion Artillery before recruiting a mounted company that became part of the 2nd Florida Cavalry. From 1863 until the war's end, Dickison defended Florida's interior against attacks from the Union-occupied coast. To loyal Confederates his exploits reached near mythic proportions.

In the spring of 1864, Dickison captured the Union outposts at Welaka and Saunders, and then ambushed and forced the surrender of the Union gunboat USS *Columbine* at Horse Landing. In August 1864, he drove off a Union

cavalry force that had briefly occupied Gainesville, inflicting nearly 200 casualties. Early in 1865, Dickison skirmished with Federal forces at Braddock's Farm, where he shot and mortally wounded the commander of the enemy detachment. He then moved his force to the Gulf coast to meet another Federal threat, skirmishing with the Federals at Station Number 4. While Dickison's efforts ensured that the interior of Florida remained in Confederate hands, he could do nothing to delay the inexorable collapse of the Confederacy, and he surrendered his command at Waldo on May 20, 1865.

To learn more, see: *J.J. Dickison: Swamp Fox of the Confederacy* by John J. Koblas, North Star Press of St. Cloud, Inc., 2000.

the pursuit by the Home Guard. The skirmish resulted in the death of two of the Home Guard and two others mortally wounded. The Union force suffered two dead and four wounded. Once across the river, the Union force attacked the Holly Plantation and then headed for the Federal garrison at St. Augustine. The 2nd Florida Cavalry, under the command of Captain J.J. Dickison, pursued the Union force to St. Augustine forcing them to abandon the property they had seized during the raid. Each fall, the Ocklawaha River Raid Reenactment, including battle reenactments and other activities, commemorates the event at the Florida Carriage Museum & Resort in Weirsdale.

SILVER RIVER MUSEUM & ENVIRONMENTAL EDUCATION CENTER
1445 NE 58th Avenue
352.236.5401
www.marion.k12.fl.us/district/srm/index.cfm

This museum is located within the Silver River State Park and is operated by the Marion County School District in cooperation with the park. The "American Civil War in Marion County" exhibit case features period objects, including a small iron cannon and a number of artillery projectiles, along with soldiers' equipment.

Orange Springs

ORANGE SPRINGS COMMUNITY CHURCH AND CEMETERY
State Road 315 and Church Street
352.546.5952

Constructed in c.1852, the land for the church and cemetery was donated by local businessman John W. Pearson, who also donated the materials for the church's construction. During the Civil War, Pearson organized, equipped and commanded the "Ocklawaha Rangers", a unit of local residents, which fought at the Battle of Olustee and later became a company in the 9th Florida Infantry. Pearson's machine shop in Orange Springs also manufactured artillery and refurbished firearms for the Confederate

military. While serving as lieutenant colonel, Pearson was severely wounded at the Battle of Globe Tavern, Virginia in August 1864. While en route back to Orange Springs the following month, he died in Georgia from his wounds, and was buried there. Local tradition holds that the Orange Springs Community Church served as a Confederate hospital during the war. The cemetery contains the remains of both Confederate and Union soldiers, and a memorial monument for Pearson is located there.

── Orange County ──
Orlando

CONFEDERATE MONUMENT
Lake Eola Park
195 North Rosalind Avenue

Dedicated in 1911 by the United Daughters of the Confederacy, this Georgia marble monument was erected in memory of the soldiers, sailors, and statesmen of the Confederacy. The ladies of the local UDC chapter amassed $2,500 for this memorial by sponsoring many strawberry and ice cream festivals. Florida Attorney General Park Trammell, who later became governor, was the speaker for

the dedication. Originally placed at the intersection of Central Boulevard and Magnolia Avenue, it was moved to its present location in 1917 to resolve a traffic hazard issue.

Confederate Monument, Orlando.
(Image courtesy of William Lees, Florida Public Archaeology Network)

GREENWOOD CEMETERY
1603 Greenwood Street
407.246.2616
www.cityoforlando.net/greenwood

Established in 1880 and purchased by the City of Orlando in 1892, this cemetery

contains both Confederate and Union sections. Over 100 Confederate veterans and nearly 100 Union veterans are interred in the cemetery. Among the Confederate veterans is William H. Jewell, who served in the 21st Mississippi Infantry and later on the staff of Lieutenant General Wade Hampton, and, in the postwar period, as a Florida legislator and Mayor of Orlando from 1907 to 1910. The Union section of the cemetery contains a monument erected by the Grand Army of the Republic, a Union veteran's organization.

── Osceola County ──
St. Cloud

ST. CLOUD HERITAGE MUSEUM
1012 Massachusetts Avenue
407.957.7587
www.stcloudheritagemuseum.com

Located in the 1922 Veterans Memorial Library, the museum contains exhibits on the history and founding of this community. St. Cloud's history is linked closely with the Grand Army of the Republic (GAR), the largest organization of Union veterans of the Civil War. While searching for a setting in which to locate a Union veteran's retirement colony, the Seminole Land and Investment Company acquired 35,000 acres of land here in 1909. Lured by the favorable climate, GAR members purchased 25 x 150' lots for $50, sight unseen. Sleeping on cots in old army tents while they built their homes, the community had a population of more than 2,000 within a few years, and in 1911 the Florida legislature granted a charter of incorporation. In 1914, the Grand Army of the Republic Memorial Hall was constructed at 1101 Massachusetts Avenue as a memorial to Union army veterans, and today is considered one of the best preserved GAR halls in the country. The museum's collections include early colony records, names and obituaries for the more than 350 Union veterans interred in Mt. Peace Cemetery, and GAR memorabilia, as well as numerous images and objects from the city's early history.

── Polk County ──

Bartow

OAK HILL CEMETERY
300 Block of West Parker Street

This cemetery contains the remains of nearly 60 Confederate veterans including Jacob Summerlin and Evander McIver Law. Jacob Summerlin was a successful cattle businessman who was known as the "Cattle King" of South Florida, and as the "King of the Crackers", a term applied to Florida cowmen. During the Civil War, Summerlin served as Chief Beef Quartermaster in the Commissary Department, and was the primary supplier of Florida beef to the Confederacy. His cracker cowmen drove the cattle north to holding pens at Baldwin in Duval County and other railheads for eventual transport to the Confederate armies. A native of South Carolina, Evander McIver Law was in Alabama at the outbreak of the Civil War and served as a captain with the Alabama troops that assisted in the seizure of the Pensacola Navy Yard and adjacent forts in early 1861. By 1865, Law had been promoted to major general and had led his troops in many of the major battles of the war in the eastern theater. After the Civil War, Law eventually moved to Bartow in 1893 to establish the South Florida Military Institute. Hundreds of mourners attended Law's funeral procession to Oak Hill Cemetery on November 2, 1920, and all of Polk County's businesses and schools closed early on that day. A small stone monument in downtown Bartow marks the site of Law's home.

POLK COUNTY HISTORICAL MUSEUM
100 East Main Street
863.534.4386
or toll free 1.800.780.5346 ext. 4386
www.polkcountymuseum.org

Located in the restored 1908 Old Polk County Courthouse, the museum contains exhibits on local and regional history, including a Civil War exhibit with period objects. The Polk County

Confederate Monument, Lakeland.
(Image courtesy of William Lees, Florida Public Archaeology Network)

Historical & Genealogical Library, located in the east wing of the building, is one of the largest such collections in the state. On the building's grounds is a monument for Company E of the 7th Florida Infantry erected in 1982 by the Sons of Confederate Veterans. Known as the "South Florida Bulldogs", this unit of local men served in the western theater from 1862 to 1865. The names of the many engagements that they participated in are listed on the monument.

Fort Meade

FORT MEADE HISTORICAL MUSEUM
1 North Tecumseh Avenue
863.285.7474

Located in the restored c.1885 Old Fort Meade School House, this museum features an extensive collection of area artifacts. During the Civil War, Fort Meade was an important Confederate cattle-driving center. In 1864, several Union raids from their post at Fort Myers were directed at Fort Meade. One raid led to a skirmish at Bowlegs Creek south of Fort Meade in April 1864. One Confederate soldier was killed and another was wounded. While the Union troops suffered no casualties, they did not continue their advance on Fort Meade. In May 1864, a larger Union force of over 200 men burned and sacked Fort Meade. They captured seven Confederate prisoners and confiscated more than 1,000 cattle. Nearly 100 Unionist refugees also returned with them to Fort Myers.

Lakeland

CONFEDERATE MONUMENT
Munn Park
Tennessee Avenue and Main Street

Located in the center of downtown Lakeland's main public space, this monument made of Georgia marble was erected in 1910. The local United Daughters of the Confederacy chapter raised the $1,750 for the construction of the 24-foot tall structure by holding cake and lemonade sales.

── Seminole County ──

Geneva

GENEVA CEMETERY
240 1st Street
www.usgennet.org/usa/fl/county/seminole/Geneva/Cemteries.htm

Convicted Lincoln conspirator and Alabama native, Lewis Thornton Powell enlisted in the Hamilton Blues Company, 2nd Florida Infantry in May, 1861. Wounded at the Battle of Gettysburg on July 2, 1863, Union soldiers hospitalized Powell in Baltimore. Escaping from there in early September, Powell found his way to Virginia where he joined up with Mosby's Raiders. In early 1865, Powell relocated to Baltimore where he met John Wilkes Booth. Powell's role in the Lincoln Conspiracy was significant. He severely wounded Secretary of State William Seward in an assassination attempt on April 14, 1865. Arrested on April 17, Powell received a guilty sentence from the Military Commission and was hung on July 7, 1865. Originally buried near the gallows, Smithsonian Institution employees found Powell's skull in their collection in 1992. Family members interred the skull in the Geneva Cemetery in 1994 near the grave of his mother, Patience Caroline Powell. Seventeen Civil War soldiers, one of whom served with the Union, are buried in the Geneva Cemetery. Powell's grave in the cemetery is on the right, approximately one-third of the way to the back.

Brevard County

Cocoa

THE FLORIDA HISTORICAL SOCIETY
435 Brevard Avenue
321.690.1971
www.myfloridahistory.org

Founded in 1856 in St. Augustine, the primary mission of the Florida Historical Society is to collect, preserve, and publish materials relating to the history of Florida and its peoples. After a period of inactivity during the Civil War and Reconstruction, it resumed operation in 1902. The society publishes the *Florida Historical Quarterly* and maintains the Library of Florida History, an extensive collection of historical documents, maps, and photographs. The collection contains numerous Civil War documents, including the papers of Captain Francis P. Fleming of the 2nd Florida Infantry and 1st Florida Cavalry and Florida governor from 1889 to 1893, and the papers of Mary Martha Reid who served as the matron of the Florida Hospital in Richmond, Virginia.

Volusia County

DeLeon Springs

DE LEON SPRINGS STATE PARK
601 Ponce de Leon Boulevard
386.985.4212
www.floridastateparks.org/deleonsprings

In April 1864, a Union army expedition of almost 1,000 men from the 17th Connecticut Infantry, the 75th Ohio Mounted Infantry, and the 35th U.S. Colored Infantry, under the command of Brigadier General William Birney, moved into Volusia County to disrupt Confederate supply lines and destroy supply sources. One of the objectives of Birney's Raid was Spring Garden Plantation (now De Leon Springs State Park)

where three cotton gins and a gristmill with four grinding stones for producing corn meal had been constructed. The mill and gins were all powered by an undershot water wheel supplied by a large natural spring. The Union soldiers destroyed the plantation and the gristmill machinery was thrown into the spring. The water wheel was reconstructed in 1999 and is now part of a restaurant at the park.

New Smyrna Beach

During the Civil War, New Smyrna (the word Beach was added to the city's name in 1947) was an active area for blockade running and salt production. Several military actions took place there. In March 1862, a Union navy raiding force from the USS *Penguin* and the USS *Henry Andrew* was attacked at the Old Stone Wharf by Confederate soldiers of the 3rd Florida Infantry. The Union force suffered eight killed, several wounded and three taken prisoner. The Confederate force reported no casualties. An escaped slave who had guided the Union force was also captured and hanged. In July 1863, the Union navy returned to New Smyrna when the USS *Oleander* and the USS *Beauregard* quietly slipped into the Indian River and anchored opposite the town. In what the Confederates considered retaliation for the earlier Union defeat, the Union ships shelled the community and then sent a landing force ashore to burn those buildings which had escaped the shelling. After destroying large quantities of cotton and several vessels to prevent their capture, the community's residents fled to the nearby woods. In May 1864, a column of Union troops under the command of Brigadier General William Birney entered New Smyrna during an expedition into Central Florida. They captured two schooners there, the *Fannie* and the *Shell*, loaded with cotton and ready to run the blockade.

NEW SMYRNA MUSEUM OF HISTORY
120 Sams Avenue
386.478.0052

Located in the restored 1925 Old Post Office building, the museum's Perimeter Gallery contains exhibits on local history, and includes Civil War artifacts. The museum also contains the Sheldon Research Library consisting of documents, books, periodicals, maps, and photographs relating to the history of New Smyrna Beach.

OLD FORT PARK
200 Block of Sams Avenue
386.424.2175
www.cityofnsb.com/index.aspx?nid=129

This city park contains massive coquina stone ruins known locally as the "Old Fort" but which are most likely the remnants of an 18th century British period residential or commercial structure. In the 1850s, a large wooden hotel with about 60 rooms was constructed by John and Jane Sheldon on top of the old coquina foundation. During the Union navy's bombardment of the community in July 1863, the Sheldon Hotel was destroyed by the explosion of gunpowder that had been stored in the cellar. After the Civil War, the Sheldon family returned to New Smyrna and rebuilt their hotel on top of the ruins. The hotel remained standing until 1896 when it was torn down.

Imported European-made musket and Confederate canteen.
(Images courtesy of the Museum of Florida History),
Union brass spurs. *(Maple Leaf collection, Image courtesy of the Florida Bureau of Arhaeological Research and the U.S. Army)*

—— Citrus County ——

Homosassa

YULEE SUGAR MILL RUINS HISTORIC STATE PARK
State Road 490
352.795.3817
www.floridastateparks.org/yuleesugarmill

David Levy Yulee, one of Florida's first United States Senators and the first Jewish member of that body, operated a 5,100-acre plantation on this site. Constructed in 1851 using expensive machinery shipped down from New York, the Yulee Sugar Mill operated until 1864, supplying sugar, syrup and molasses to Confederate troops during the Civil War. After Florida seceded from the Union, Yulee resigned his Senate seat and remained in Florida until the end of the war. In May 1864, Union troops destroyed Yulee's Margarita Plantation home and his stockpile of supplies at Homosassa, but failed to locate and destroy the mill. The mill, however, was abandoned and did not resume operations. Imprisoned at the end of the war for his support of the Confederacy, upon his release Yulee returned to his Florida railroad interests. The park contains the ruins of the once-thriving sugar plantation, including the steam boiler, crushing machinery, and large cooking kettles.

Inverness

THE OLD COURTHOUSE HERITAGE MUSEUM
1 Courthouse Square
352.341.6488
www.cccourthouse.org

Formed in 1963, the Citrus County Historical Society, Inc. exists to "preserve and further the knowledge of the history and pre-history of Citrus County and nearby areas" and, since 1985, has been located in the restored 1912 Old Citrus County Courthouse. In the local history gallery, the museum contains an exhibit on the role of Citrus County in the Civil War. The exhibit includes interpretation of Florida in the Civil War, local Home Guard units, blockade runners, David Levy Yulee's sugar mill, and the burning of the Yulee plantation home by Union troops.

Yulee Sugar Mill, Homosassa. *(Image courtesy of William Lees, Florida Public Archaeology Network)*

David Levy Yulee, U.S. Senator from Florida.
(Image courtesy of the State Archives of Florida)

David Levy Yulee

The first Jewish member of the United States Senate, David Levy Yulee was a major political and economic figure in mid-nineteenth century Florida. Born David Levy in the Virgin Islands in 1810, his family eventually settled in Florida. He served in the Florida Territorial Legislative Council, was a delegate to the 1838 Constitutional Convention, and served as territorial delegate to the U.S. Congress. In 1845, he became one of the new state's first senators. His marriage in 1846 probably contributed to his conversion to Christianity and surname change to Yulee. In addition to politics, Yulee operated a sugar plantation, and became active in railroad development, particularly the building of the Florida Railroad.

Yulee resigned from the Senate following Florida's secession in 1861. His sugar mill at Homosassa supplied sugar, syrup and molasses to the Confederacy until May 1864, when Union forces burned his Margarita Plantation home and the mill ceased production. He held no political office in the Confederacy, and spent much time and effort fighting the state and Confederate governments over the impressment of his agricultural products and the seizure of iron from his rail line. Imprisoned by Union authorities at Fort Pulaski, Georgia for a time after the war, he returned to Florida and attempted to rebuild his economic interests. He died in 1886.

To learn more, see: "David L. Yulee, Florida's First Senator" by Leon Huhner, in *Jews In the South,* edited by Leonard Dinnerstein and Mary Dale Palsson, Louisiana State University Press, 1973.

— Hernando County —

Brooksville

In July 1864, a Union force of 240 soldiers from the 2nd U.S. Colored Infantry and 2nd Florida Union Cavalry landed near Bayport and advanced towards Brooksville to destroy Confederate supplies. For a week, the Union force raided Hernando County plantations in the area surrounding Brooksville, skirmishing on several occasions with Confederate Home Guard troops, before falling back on Bayport. There, the Union troops boarded naval vessels for the return trip to their post at Fort Myers with several Confederate prisoners, contraband slaves, and captured cotton and livestock. In 1916, the United Daughters of the Confederacy erected a Confederate monument in Brooksville on the lawn of the Hernando County Courthouse.

MAY-STRINGER HOUSE

601 Museum Court
352.799.0129
www.hernandohistoricalmuseumassoc.com
Constructed in 1856, the May-Stringer House was the postwar residence of Frank E. Saxon who served in the "Hernando Wildcats" unit of the 3rd Florida Infantry and was badly wounded at the Battle of Perryville, Kentucky in October 1862. Today, the house is the home of the Hernando Heritage Museum, which contains over 11,000 Hernando County artifacts. Artifacts in the museum's "War Room" include items from the Civil War. The Hernando Historical Museum Association sponsors the annual Civil War Brooksville Raid Reenactment on the third weekend of January, one of the largest such events in Florida.

Spring Hill

BAYPORT PARK

4140 Cortez Road
During the Civil War, the port community of Bayport was an active area for blockade running. In April 1863, an expedition of Union sailors in seven launches and cutters entered the harbor

Confederate Monument, Brooksville.
(Image courtesy of William Lees, Florida Public Archaeology Network)

where six blockade runners were in port. Four of these vessels fled into the bayou where they grounded on the banks while a fifth vessel, the *Helen*, was burned by the raiding force. As the Union boats armed with howitzers headed for the sixth vessel, a schooner loaded with cotton, they exchanged fire with the Confederate battery of two cannons at Bayport and Confederate riflemen along the shore. Before they reached the Confederate vessel, it burst into flames, presumably to prevent its capture, and the Union force withdrew. The Union force suffered one wounded while the Confederate losses were one killed and three wounded. In September 1863, a Union force of several ships returned to Bayport to destroy a blockade runner, but the Confederates set fire to it and to a cotton warehouse before the Union navy could attack. A historical marker at Bayport Park discusses the Civil War history of Bayport. The Confederate cannon battery site can still be seen on a wooded point north of the pier at Bayport Park. In 2009, the Florida Public Archaeology Network began a project to document and map Confederate shipwrecks at Bayport. Hernando Past, a local historic preservation society, plans to install interpretive kiosks on the Civil War at Bayport Park.

— Hillsborough County —

Egmont Key

EGMONT KEY LIGHTHOUSE

Egmont Key State Park
727.893.2627
www.floridastateparks.org/egmontkey
The present Egmont Key Lighthouse was constructed in 1858 to replace the earlier 1848 lighthouse. Early in the Civil War, Confederate authorities ordered that the lighthouse lens and other equipment be removed for safekeeping. In August 1861, they were removed to Tampa, and then, in April 1862, to Brooksville. In November 1861, Union naval forces occupied Egmont Key and, for the remainder of the war, used the island as a base of operations for the East Gulf Blockading Squadron. They constructed several structures near the lighthouse and a gun battery on the shore facing Tampa. The lighthouse was used by Union forces as a watchtower for locating Confederate blockade runners. In 1864, a hospital for 30 patients was also constructed. Throughout the war, Egmont Key served as a staging area for Union raids and attacks on Tampa and present-day Pinellas County. By February 1862, Egmont Key was also being used as a refuge for runaway slaves and Florida Unionists fleeing Confederate persecution, and for housing Confederate prisoners. Nearly 200 refugees reportedly stayed on the island in 1863 while awaiting transport to Union-held areas. A cemetery was established just south of the lighthouse for the Union sailors who died while on duty there, the great majority from yellow fever. In 1909, their remains were moved to the St. Augustine National Cemetery as part of the nationwide effort to consolidate military burials. During World War II, the top portion of the lighthouse was removed and replaced with a modern beacon on a concrete deck.

Plant City

EAST HILLSBOROUGH HISTORICAL SOCIETY MUSEUM
605 North Collins Street
813.757.9226
www.rootsweb.ancestry.com/~flqgbac/ehhs.html

Located in the restored 1914 Plant City High School building, the East Hillsborough Historical Society is dedicated to the preservation of the historical and cultural heritage of Plant City and eastern Hillsborough County. The Society maintains a museum and the Quintilla Geer Bruton Archives Center which contains an extensive collection of books, census records, newspapers and other documents, as well as historic photographs. On the building's grounds is a Confederate "Cow Cavalry" unit monument erected in 2007 by the United Daughters of the Confederacy. Formed to defend Florida cattle herds from Union raiders, the names of area residents who served in the unit are listed on the monument.

Tampa

During the Civil War, Tampa was an active area for Confederate blockade running and salt production, and was blockaded by Union vessels throughout the war. Several military actions also took place there. On June 30-July 1, 1862, Tampa was shelled by the Union gunboat USS *Sagamore* after Confederate forces refused an ultimatum to surrender. The Confederates returned fire from their battery at Fort Brooke but the Union gunboat was out of range. Little damage was done to Tampa or Fort Brooke, and no casualties were reported. On October 16-17, 1863, Tampa and Fort Brooke were again shelled by the Union gunboats USS *Tahoma* and USS *Adela* as a cover for a Union raiding force which burned two blockade runners in the Hillsborough River. As the raiders attempted to return to their ships on October 18, they were attacked at Ballast Point by a Confederate force and, after a sharp skirmish with casualties on both sides, withdrew to their vessels. Before leaving the area, the Union navy sent another raiding party to destroy a large salt making facility at the head of Tampa Bay near the east end of the present-day Courtney Campbell Causeway. On May 6-7, 1864, a Union force of several hundred men from the 2nd U.S. Colored Infantry, 2nd Florida Union Cavalry, and Union navy occupied Tampa after most of the Confederate defenders were withdrawn to reinforce the hard-pressed army in Virginia. After taking some prisoners, capturing a sloop loaded with cotton, and destroying the Fort Brooke battery, the Union forces returned to their ships. Union forces continued to raid Tampa Bay area saltworks throughout the remainder of the war.

Confederate Monument, Tampa.
(Image courtesy of William Lees, Florida Public Archaeology Network)

CONFEDERATE MONUMENT
Pierce Street

Originally located on the grounds of the Old Hillsborough County Courthouse, the monument was erected in 1911 by the United Daughters of the Confederacy. In 1952, the monument was moved to its current location upon the completion of the new courthouse building. A City Historical Marker for "Memoria in Aeterna, 1911 – Hillsborough County's Confederate Monument" is located a few steps away from the monument and provides information on its history.

FORT BROOKE BATTERY
University of Tampa
813.253.3333
www.ut.edu/history

Mounted in Plant Park are two Civil War 24-pounder cannons, which were originally part of a Confederate battery at Fort Brooke. In 1891, while constructing the Tampa Bay Hotel, Henry B. Plant had the cannons salvaged from the Fort Brooke site and relocated to the hotel grounds. Originally established in 1824, Fort Brooke was located on the east bank of the Hillsborough River where it flows into Hillsborough Bay. At the beginning of the Civil War, Confederate troops occupied Fort Brooke to protect Tampa and the surrounding areas from Union invasion and to facilitate the blockade runners departing and entering Tampa. The fort was bombarded by Union warships in June-July 1862 and in October 1863. In May 1864, Union forces temporarily occupied Tampa and captured Fort Brooke. Before departing, they destroyed the fort, disabled its 24-pounder cannons, and hauled away its smaller cannons. Today, nothing remains of Fort Brooke, the main area of which is under the Tampa Convention Center.

USS *Sagamore* Shell Monument,
Oaklawn Cemetery, Tampa.
(Image courtesy of William Lees, Florida Public Archaeology Network)

OAKLAWN CEMETERY
606 East Harrison Street

This cemetery contains the remains of over 60 Confederate veterans, including Major John T. Lesley who organized the local Confederate company, the "Sunny South Guards", at the outbreak of the war. Lesley later served as a company commander of the "Cow Cavalry" which defended Florida cattle herds from Union raids. Also buried in the cemetery is businessman James McKay, Sr. who was Tampa's most active Civil War blockade runner. He also served as commissary officer of the Fifth Florida District responsible for supplying the Confederate armies with South Florida cattle. His son, James McKay, Jr., served as a captain in the Florida "Cow Cavalry" and is also buried in this cemetery. The cemetery contains several small Civil War monuments. A small marble marker at the grave of Darwin B.Givens states that, as a small boy, he alerted Tampa of the 1864 Union invasion with the cry "the devils are coming." A small stone marker notes that an 8-inch shell landed in the cemetery during the bombardment of Tampa by the USS *Sagamore* on June 30-July 1, 1862. Another small stone marker was erected in 1975 by the United Daughters of the Confederacy in memory of the Confederate soldiers and sailors interred here, and another was placed here for Union soldiers by the Daughters of Union Veterans.

Cattle and Cow Cavalry

In the years prior to the Civil War, cattle raising had developed into a significant industry in southern Florida and, by 1862, it was estimated that Florida had more than 650,000 head of cattle. In 1863, Pleasants Woodson White was appointed the commissary officer for the state. One of his goals was the acquisition of cattle to feed the Confederacy's armies, especially after the capture of Vicksburg cut off the supply of cattle from Texas. In an effort to protect the Florida herds against Union forces, the Confederate government formed the 1st Florida Special Cavalry Battalion, popularly known as the Cow Cavalry, in 1864.

That year, small-scale Union raids to disrupt cattle supplies became common in south Florida, and expeditions were launched to the Peace River Valley and the cattle-driving center of Fort Meade. Emboldened, Union forces also attacked Tampa and Fort Brooke. In February 1865, the Cow Cavalry launched an attack on the Union post at Fort Myers. While unsuccessful, the attack did lead to the post's evacuation the following month. By then, however, the cattle driving season had ended for the year

Jacob Summerlin, Confederate "Cattle King."
(Image courtesy of the State Archives of Florida)

and the war was nearly over. The hope of Florida beef feeding large numbers of Confederates had not been fulfilled.

To learn more, see: "Cow Cavalry: Munnerlyn's Battalion in Florida, 1864-1865" by Robert A. Taylor, *The Florida Historical Quarterly,* Vol. 65, No. 2, October 1986.

TAMPA BLOCKADE RUNNERS AND BATTLE OF BALLAST POINT HISTORICAL MARKERS
1101 West Sligh Avenue, and Corner of Bayshore and Gandy Boulevards

A City Historical Marker for "Union Raiders Burn Tampa Blockade Runners" and a County Historical Marker for "Battlefield" tell the story of the Hillsborough River Raid and the ensuing Battle of Ballast Point. In October 1863, as the Union vessels USS *Tahoma* and USS *Adela* bombarded Fort Brooke and Tampa, a raiding party of 106 sailors with two local Unionist guides commanded by Acting Master Thomas Harris landed at Gadsden Point and made their way northward. In the Hillsborough River near present-day Lowry Park, they located two blockade runners owned

by James McKay, Sr. The *Scottish Chief* and the *Kate Dale* were burned by the Union raiders, along with the 167 bales of cotton on them. They also took seven Confederate prisoners. The Confederates set a third vessel, the *A.B. Noyes,* on fire to prevent its capture. The raiders then proceeded to Ballast Point where they were attacked by 40 Confederate troops commanded by Captain John Westcott of the 2nd Florida Infantry Battalion as they embarked to return to their ships. In the ensuing skirmish, the Union force suffered three dead, ten wounded, and five taken prisoner while the Confederates lost six killed and an undetermined number of wounded. In 2008, underwater archaeologists from the Florida Aquarium in Tampa located the remains of the *Kate Dale* in the

Hillsborough River near Lowry Park, and in 2009 the remains of the *Scottish Chief* were located further down river. An exhibit at the Florida Aquarium on local Civil War shipwrecks is in the planning stages.

Colt Navy Revolver with Florida and Confederate currency.
(Image courtesy of the Museum of Florida History)

Union Monument and Union graves, Woodlawn Cemetery, Tampa.
(Image courtesy of William Lees, Florida Public Archaeology Network)

WOODLAWN CEMETERY
3412 Ola Avenue

This cemetery contains side by side plots of Confederate and Union veterans each with their own monument. The Confederate monument was erected in 1913 by the United Confederate Veterans and lists the names of the 30 veterans buried there. The Union monument was erected by the Grand Army of the Republic's Woman's Relief Corps, and is surrounded by 21 marked veterans' graves. Among the Union veterans buried elsewhere in this cemetery are two Medal of Honor recipients, one from the Battle of Gettysburg and the other from the Siege of Vicksburg.

Florida Brigade in the Western Theater

In April 1862, the 1st Florida Battalion fought in the Battle of Shiloh, where it suffered heavy casualties. In the aftermath of that battle, a new 1st Florida Regiment was established, consisting of the survivors of the Florida Battalion and six new companies. Soon other Florida regiments were sent to reinforce the Confederate army in Tennessee, including the 3rd, 4th, 6th, and 7th Florida Infantry and the 1st Florida Cavalry. They took part in the 1862 Confederate invasion of Kentucky, with the 1st and 3rd Regiments being heavily engaged at the Battle of Perryville in October. After Perryville, the 1st and 3rd Regiments were consolidated together and, along with the 4th Regiment, suffered heavy casualties in the subsequent Battle of Stones River (Second Murfreesboro),

after which they participated in the Siege of Jackson.

In September 1863, the Florida troops fought with the Army of Tennessee in inflicting a severe defeat on the Federals at the Battle of Chickamauga. After this battle, the various Florida units were merged into a single Florida Brigade, commanded by Brigadier General Jesse Finley. They then took part in the unsuccessful siege of Chattanooga and the Confederate defeat at the Battle of Missionary Ridge. In 1864, they defended Atlanta and participated in the Tennessee Campaign and the disastrous Battles of Franklin and Nashville. The remnants ended the war in North Carolina in the spring of 1865, surrendering just 351 survivors.

To learn more, see: "By the Noble Daring of Her Sons: The Florida Brigade of the Army of Tennessee" by Jonathan Sheppard, Ph.D. dissertation, Florida State University, 2008. Available online at:

http://etd.lib.fsu.edu/theses/available/etd-08232008-104040/ (Pending publication, University of Alabama Press, 2012)

Corporal Seaborn Tiller, 6th Florida Infantry.
(Image courtesy of the Museum of Florida History)

—— Pinellas County ——
St. Petersburg

GREENWOOD CEMETERY
**Dr. Martin Luther King Jr. Street South
and 11th Avenue South**
www.historicgreenwood.com

Often called the "Veteran's Cemetery" due to the number of Civil War soldiers and sailors buried here, this cemetery contains the remains of at least 100 Confederate and Union veterans. In 1900, two monuments were constructed at the center of the cemetery in honor of each side. The Confederate monument was erected by "Confederate Veterans and Friends", while the Union monument was erected by the Grand Army of the Republic, a Union veteran's organization.

MIRANDA HOME STATE HISTORICAL MARKER
4th Street South and Oakdale Street South

A State Historical Marker for the "Miranda Home" is located in the vicinity of the home of Abel Miranda who, with his brothers-in-law John and William Bethell, ran a successful fishing operation in Big Bayou. Miranda and the Bethells were prominent Confederate supporters who harassed local Unionists. In order to put a halt to the persecution of Union sympathizers in the area, a force of Union navy sailors from their base at Egmont Key, guided by local civilian Unionists, raided the area in February 1862. Miranda's home was first shelled by the Union navy, and then the raiding force sacked and burned the house. The Confederates' boats were seized, their farm animals were killed, and their gardens and orange groves were destroyed. There were no casualties. Following this destruction, Miranda and the Bethells fled to Tampa where John Bethell joined the 7th Florida Infantry as a lieutenant.

Florida Brigade in the Eastern Theater

The 2nd Florida Infantry Regiment reached Virginia in July 1861, barely missing the Battle of First Bull Run (First Manassas). It fought in the Peninsula Campaign/Seven Days Battles in front of Richmond in the late spring and summer of 1862 as part of the newly-organized Army of Northern Virginia. At the Battle of Seven Pines, Virginia in May 1862, the unit performed heroically in capturing a Union artillery battery but suffered heavy casualties. The Floridians fought at the Battles of Second Bull Run (Second Manassas) and Antietam (Sharpsburg) in that summer and fall, as well as at the Battle of Fredericksburg in December.

In the summer of 1862 they were joined by the 5th and 8th Florida Regiments, and before the end of the year a unified Florida Brigade was created under the command of Brigadier General Edward Perry. The unit fought at the Battle of Chancellorsville in April-May 1863 and at the Battle of Gettysburg that summer. With Perry sidelined by illness, Colonel David Lang commanded the brigade during the latter campaign, during which they launched an assault in support of Pickett's Charge and suffered heavy losses.

The following year the brigade took part in the Overland Campaign, losing Perry to a wound at the Battle of the Wilderness. By the end of the Overland Campaign, reinforcements from Florida commanded by Brigadier General Joseph Finegan reached the Army of Northern Virginia and joined their fellow Floridians. The additional troops were organized as the 9th, 10th, and 11th Florida Regiments, and Finegan assumed command of the Florida Brigade. At the Battle of Cold Harbor, Virginia in June 1864, the Floridians again performed heroically, driving back a Union attack that had briefly penetrated the Confederate lines.

For the remainder of 1864 and early 1865, the Floridians suffered in the siege lines around Petersburg. In March 1865, Finegan returned to Florida, and Brigadier General Theodore Brevard commanded the brigade during the evacuation of Richmond and Petersburg and the subsequent retreat westward until his capture at Sailor's Creek on April 6. Colonel Lang commanded the survivors who surrendered at Appomattox three days later.

To learn more, see: *A Small but Spartan Band: The Florida Brigade in Lee's Army of Northern Virginia* by Zack C. Waters and James C. Edmonds, University of Alabama Press, 2010.

"The Florida Brigade at Cold Harbor" June 3, 1864, Cold Harbor, Virginia.
(Artist: Jackson Walker, Image courtesy of the Florida National Guard)

— Hendry County —

LaBelle

FORT THOMPSON STATE HISTORICAL MARKER
State Road 80

A State Historical Marker is located at the site of Fort Thompson, which was constructed in the late 1830s on the Caloosahatchee River for use as a military supply post during the Second Seminole War. During the Civil War, the Confederates used this area to raise cattle and, in January 1864, a Union scouting expedition from Fort Myers skirmished with Confederate pickets at this site. In February 1865, Fort Thompson was used as the staging area for the Confederate "Cow Cavalry" forces who conducted an unsuccessful attack on Fort Myers. Captain Francis Asbury Hendry, who had led a company of Confederate troops in the February 1865 attack on Fort Myers, acquired the property after the war, in 1879. He established a cattle ranch there, and a town soon grew along its western boundary. By the early 1900's, the former fort site had become the cattle and citrus town of LaBelle.

— Lee County —

Fort Myers

Established by the U.S. Army in 1850 as a military supply post, Fort Myers became the principal base for military operations into the Big Cypress Swamp during the Third Seminole War of 1855-1858. With the end of the war in 1858, the post was abandoned. In December 1863, a small Union force occupied Useppa Island, and in January 1864 Union troops reoccupied Fort Myers as a base of operations for raids into the interior to disrupt Confederate cattle supplies and to provide a refuge for escaped slaves, Confederate deserters, and Unionist refugees. In response, the Confederate government established a military unit to defend Florida cattle herds composed of South Florida residents, known as the "Cow Cavalry." After a series of destructive Union raids

Seminoles

In the first 60 years of the nineteenth century, the Seminole Indians fought three wars against American expansion into their territory. A few Seminoles, led by Tiger Tail and the aged Sam Jones, remained in south Florida at the outbreak of the Civil War. A concern at the time was that the remaining Indians might create unrest along the southern frontier. In the latter part of 1862, false rumors circulated that the Seminoles had murdered several settlers in the Peace River Valley.

Captain Francis A. Hendry (center left, standing) with group of Seminole Indians, post Civil War. *(Image courtesy of the State Archives of Florida)*

A state agent met with Sam Jones in 1863 and became convinced that the Seminoles planned to take no part in the fighting. At another meeting in early 1864, the Indians again proclaimed a desire for neutrality, but at about the same time another group visited Union-occupied Fort Myers. Likely they hoped to maintain good relations with both sides. A dubious claim made during this period was that more than 60 Seminoles had enlisted to serve in a Confederate company. Nothing more was heard of this unit and it most likely never actually existed. The end of the war came in the spring of 1865, and true to their word the Seminoles had not become involved in the conflict.

To learn more, see: "Unforgotten Threat: Florida Seminoles in the Civil War" by Robert A. Taylor, *The Florida Historical Quarterly*, Vol. 69, No. 3, January 1991.

launched from Fort Myers in 1864 and early 1865, a force of Confederate "Cow Cavalry" attacked the post in February 1865. The attack was repulsed with light casualties for both sides. Despite the Confederate failure to capture the post, Union authorities evacuated Fort Myers in March 1865, and temporarily moved some of the troops to Punta Rassa before completely withdrawing from the area.

FORT MYERS ATTACK STATE HISTORICAL MARKER
Between Southwest Florida Museum of History & Lee County Library

A State Historical Marker for "The Attack On Fort Myers" contains details on the Confederate attempt to capture

Fort Myers. On February 20, 1865, a Confederate force of some 275 men of Florida's "Cow Cavalry" commanded by Major William Footman launched an attack with one artillery piece on the Union garrison at Fort Myers. The Union force, with two cannons, consisted of approximately 250 men of the 2nd Florida Union Cavalry and the 2nd U.S. Colored Infantry commanded by Captain James Doyle. After surprising and attacking Union pickets and a laundry detail outside the fort, Major Footman demanded the surrender of the fort. The demand was refused and, after a lengthy skirmish, the Confederate forces withdrew under cover of darkness. Casualties on both sides were light.

MONUMENT TO U. S. COLORED TROOPS

2100 Edwards Drive

Installed in 2000, the Civil War's "2nd Regiment Infantry, U. S. Colored Troops" monument is dedicated to the black Union soldiers who defended the Federal post at Fort Myers against the Confederate attack in February 1865. A single black soldier standing at ease with his rifle before a wall with a gate represents the gateway to freedom from slavery. Also known as the "Sgt. Clayton" statue for the ton of clay required to sculpt the bronze figure, the monument is located in Fort Myers' Centennial Park.

SOUTHWEST FLORIDA MUSEUM OF HISTORY

2301 Jackson Street
239.321.7430
www.swflmuseumofhistory.com

Housed in the former 1924 Atlantic Coastline Railroad Depot, the Museum contains exhibits on the history of Fort Myers and Southwest Florida, an extensive local artifact collection, and an archival collection with photos, maps, and other documents available for researchers. Civil War activity in the area

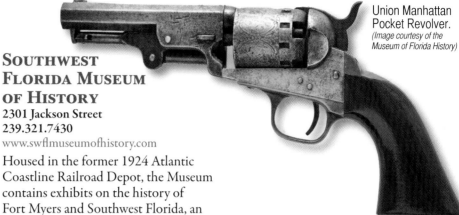

Union Manhattan Pocket Revolver.
(Image courtesy of the Museum of Florida History)

is interpreted through exhibits featuring period artifacts and a scale model of the February 1865 Confederate attack on the Federal post at Fort Myers.

Union Black Soldiers Monument, Fort Myers.
(Image courtesy of William Lees, Florida Public Archaeology Network)

African American Military Units in Florida

During the Union occupations of Jacksonville, Florida slaves and free blacks flocked to the protection of the Northern military. Many were sent to Beaufort, South Carolina, where three black regiments were eventually organized, with more than 1,000 recruits coming from Florida. Abolitionist Thomas Wentworth Higginson led the 1st South Carolina Colored Infantry Regiment on a raid up the St. Mary's River in January 1863, the first use of black troops in Florida. Two months later, the 1st and 2nd South Carolina Colored Infantry Regiments landed at Jacksonville, occupying the town for several weeks.

In the 1864 Olustee campaign, black regiments, including the 8th and the 35th U.S. Colored Infantry, and the famed 54th Massachusetts Infantry, comprised a large percentage of the Union force, with the latter two units protecting the defeated Union army as it retreated to Jacksonville. Black units participated in subsequent military operations in Florida, including the expedition to Marianna, the skirmish at Station No. 4, and the defense of Fort Myers. The last operation of significance was the St. Marks

expedition of March 1865, in which the 2nd and the 99th U.S. Colored Infantry played a major role in the engagement at Natural Bridge.

To learn more, see: "They Fought Like Devils: Black Troops in Florida During the Civil War" by David J. Coles, in *Florida's Heritage of Diversity: Essays in Honor of Samuel Proctor,* Sentry Press, 1997.

Private Robert J. Jones, 54th Massachusetts Infantry Regiment. Reported as wounded and missing at the Battle of Olustee and presumably died while a prisoner.
(Image courtesy of the State Archives of Florida)

First Manatee County Courthouse, Bradenton.
(Image courtesy of the Manatee County Historical Commission)

—— Manatee County ——

Bradenton

In August 1864, Union naval forces raided the Village of Manatee (now known as Bradenton) and destroyed a large saw and grist mill owned by John Curry and others. Later that same month, Union soldiers of the 2nd U.S. Colored Infantry landed at the Village of Manatee and occupied the town for several weeks. In 1924, a Confederate monument was erected in Bradenton by the United Daughters of the Confederacy on the grounds of the Manatee County Courthouse.

CURRY SETTLEMENT HOMES
1300 Block of 4th Avenue East
941.746.2035
www.reflectionsofmanatee.com

Originally from Key West, John W. Curry relocated his family to Manatee in 1860 and constructed several houses close to the Manatee Mineral Spring before and following the Civil War. During the Civil War, Curry sold a number of vessels to the Confederacy for use as blockade runners, and he and other family members served in the local Home Guard militia. One of his sons, Samuel G. Curry, served in the 7th Florida Infantry and the Confederate navy, including service on the gunboat CSS *Chattahoochee* on the Apalachicola River. One of the Curry houses was used by Union troops as officers quarters during

their 1864 occupation of Manatee, while the infantry encamped on the Curry property. At the end of the war, Curry played a major role in assisting Confederate Secretary of State Judah P. Benjamin during his flight through the area to England. Two of the Curry Settlement Homes are in the process of being restored for public interpretation.

FIRST MANATEE COUNTY COURTHOUSE
1404 Manatee Avenue East
941.749.7165
www.manateeclerk.com/historical/
ManateeVillage.aspx

Constructed in 1860, this small wood framed building is believed to be the oldest remaining county courthouse built for that purpose in Florida. During the Civil War, the courthouse served as the political and judicial center of Manatee County which at that time also included present-day Charlotte, DeSoto, Glades, Hardee, Highlands, and Sarasota Counties. Throughout the war, the Manatee County Commission met at the courthouse in emergency sessions to distribute available food and money to families whose male members were serving in the Confederate military or who had died while in the service. In 1975, the courthouse building was relocated to the Manatee Village Historical Park where it was restored and opened as part of the Park's exhibition on Manatee County pioneer life.

MANATEE BURYING GROUND CEMETERY
15th Street East

This cemetery contains the remains of at least ten Confederate veterans and officials including three delegates to the Florida Secession Convention - Ezekiel Glazier, James G. Cooper, and Dr. John C. Pelot, as well as at least three Union veterans including Brigadier General John Riggin who served as an aide to General Ulysses S. Grant. Also buried here is blockade runner Captain Frederick Tresca who, after the fall of the Confederacy, played a major role in aiding Confederate Secretary of State Judah P. Benjamin evade capture and escape through southwest Florida to the Bahamas and then to England in 1865. Another blockade runner who assisted Benjamin in his escape, Archibald McNeill, is believed to be buried here in an unmarked grave. A State Historical Marker for the cemetery is located at the site.

MANATEE COUNTY HISTORICAL RECORDS LIBRARY
1405 4th Avenue West
941.741.4070
www.manateeclerk.com/historical/
HistoricalLibrary.aspx

Located in the restored 1918 Carnegie Library building, the library contains governmental records dating back to 1855. County historical records, some of the Civil War era, are available to researchers, including deed books, marriage licenses, probate files, court records, County Commission minute books, maps, soldiers and sailors discharge books, and records regarding the marks, brands and numbers of cattle shipped and sold in the area.

Pocketwatch carried by a Confederate soldier.
(Image courtesy of the Museum of Florida History)
Union sunglasses. *(Maple Leaf collection, Image courtesy of the Florida Bureau of Archaeological Research and the U.S. Army)*

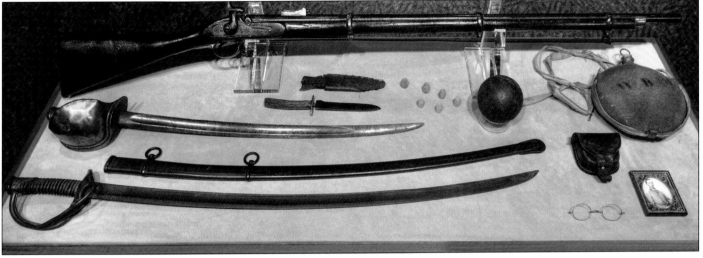

Civil War exhibit at South Florida Museum, Bradenton. *(Image courtesy of the South Florida Museum)*

SOUTH FLORIDA MUSEUM

201 10th Street West
941.746.4131
www.southfloridamuseum.org

The museum's "River Heritage Hall" presents information about the 19th century history of the region. An exhibit case of Civil War artifacts features an Enfield rifle-musket and a Union naval cutlass. A separate exhibit on medical history includes an ivory-handled Civil War period surgeon's kit that was found in the attic of an old house in Tallahassee in 1929.

Ellenton

GAMBLE PLANTATION HISTORIC STATE PARK

3708 Patten Avenue
941.723.4536
www.floridastateparks.org/gambleplantation

Major Robert Gamble began a 3,500-acre sugar plantation on this site in 1844, and constructed the Gamble Mansion and a sugar mill of brick and tabby between 1845 and 1856. The Gamble family sold the plantation in 1858, and in the spring of 1862 the Confederate government expropriated the plantation from its new

Louisiana-based owners. Blockade runner Captain Archibald McNeill became the caretaker of the plantation, and lived in the mansion until 1873. In August 1864, a Union navy raiding force destroyed the Gamble Plantation sugar mill but left the mansion untouched. With the collapse of the Confederacy, Confederate Secretary of State Judah P. Benjamin fled to Manatee County in May 1865 during his eventual escape to England. Captain McNeill assisted Benjamin in eluding the Federal troops, and Benjamin was hidden briefly at the Gamble Mansion before escaping Florida by boat. In 1925, the United Daughters of the Confederacy purchased the Gamble Mansion, which had fallen into a state of neglect and disrepair, along with 16 acres. In 1926, they donated the Gamble Mansion to the State of Florida for use as the Judah P. Benjamin Confederate Memorial, but continued to manage it until 1949. Twenty additional acres including the sugar mill ruins were purchased by the state in 2002. The only surviving antebellum plantation house in South Florida, the Gamble Mansion is decorated with period furnishings. A separate visitor center museum contains exhibit materials on the history of the plantation. The park also contains a United Daughters of the Confederacy (UDC) records and archives building, a small granite monument to Confederate veterans erected by the UDC in 1937, and the c.1885 Patten House operated by the UDC.

Gamble Plantation, Ellenton. *(Image courtesy of William Lees, Florida Public Archaeology Network)*

Cape Florida Lighthouse, Key Biscayne. *(Image courtesy of the Florida Park Service)*

Miami

CITY OF MIAMI CEMETERY
1800 NE 2nd Avenue
305.579.6938
www.miamigov.com/Parks/pages/park_
listings/cemetery.asp

Founded in 1897, Miami's oldest cemetery contains the remains of at least 66 Confederate veterans and 27 Union veterans. A Confederate monument erected by the United Daughters of the Confederacy and surrounded by Confederate graves is located in a traffic circle near the center of the cemetery. Originally erected in 1913 at the Dade County Courthouse grounds and dedicated the following year, the monument was relocated to this cemetery when a new county courthouse was constructed in 1927. The monument was heavily damaged in a subsequent hurricane, most likely in 1935, when its spire portion was broken off and never replaced. A State Historical Marker for the "Miami City Cemetery" is located at the site and provides information on its history.

Confederate Monument, Miami City Cemetery.
(Image courtesy of William Lees, Florida Public Archaeology Network)

— Miami-Dade County —

Key Biscayne

CAPE FLORIDA LIGHTHOUSE
Bill Baggs Cape Florida State Park
305.361.5811
www.floridastateparks.org/capeflorida

To protect shipping in the hazardous Straits of Florida, Congress authorized the construction of the Cape Florida Lighthouse in 1822. The first lighting occurred on December 17, 1825. In July 1836, an Indian attack in the early months of the Second Seminole War resulted in heavy damage to the tower. Rebuilt in 1846, the tower was heightened to 95 feet in 1855 under the direction of Lieutenant, later General, George Meade, the Union commander at the Battle of Gettysburg in July 1863. With the advent of the Civil War, Confederate sympathizers overwhelmed the lighthouse keeper in August 1861, damaged the central prism, and removed the reflector, rendering the lamp too dim for visibility by ships. In April 1862, a group of carpenters accompanied by troops of the 47th Pennsylvania Infantry were sent to repair the lighthouse by Union authorities. With their limited resources, they found the damage to be too extensive to repair, and the lighthouse remained darkened for the duration of the war. Lighthouse service was restored on April 15, 1866. Service was discontinued in 1878.

Union Soldier Monument, Woodlawn Park Cemetery, Miami.
(Image courtesy of Sarah Nohe, Florida Public Archaeology Network)

UNION MONUMENT

3260 SW 8th Street

Located in Woodlawn Park Cemetery, this sculptured monument of a Union soldier, which is very unusual for a Southern cemetery, was dedicated by the Grand Army of the Republic (GAR), a Union veteran's organization, in 1939. It is believed to be the southernmost location of a GAR monument in the country.

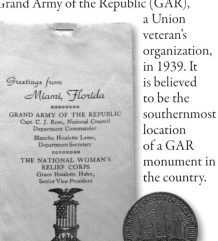

Union veterans reunion ribbon and Miami Union Monument medal, 1930s.
(Images courtesy of Frederick Gaske, Historic Preservation Services)

Flags

During the Civil War, flags served as important symbols of the two warring political entities, but also had the practical application of marking the positions of units on the battlefield.

When Florida seceded from the Union, "The Ladies Of Broward's Neck" from Duval County presented a secession flag they had made for the occasion that proclaimed: THE RIGHTS OF THE SOUTH AT ALL HAZARDS! Another secession-era flag, raised over Fort Barrancas and the Pensacola Navy Yard, was a copy of the United States flag, except that the canton contained a single large star. Later in 1861, Governor Perry chose a new state flag design, but it does not appear to have been flown and no example survives.

In its short history, the Confederate States of America adopted a number of flags. The First National flag, or Stars and Bars, was adopted in 1861. Early in the war, flags of this design were presented by women to local companies of Florida volunteers. Some companies, however, received unique banners. Perhaps the most well-known example is that of St. Augustine's Florida Independent Blues, defiantly inscribed: ANY FATE BUT SUBMISSION. As companies were organized into regiments and sent outside the state to fight, the company flags were replaced by regimental flags.

Desiring a distinctive emblem for the use of troops in the field, the Confederate military adopted the famous battle flag bearing stars on a blue St. Andrews Cross on a red

5th Florida Infantry Regiment flag.
(Image courtesy of the Museum of Florida History)

field. Most Florida regiments carried various examples of this banner, usually square-shaped but sometimes rectangular, and some emblazoned with the unit's number and battle honors. Regiments at times had to replace their flags; some were battle-damaged, retired from service and sent to the governor, while others were captured. At Gettysburg, two Florida regiments lost their colors, with the 2nd Florida Infantry's silk presentation flag being captured as the unit advanced in support of Pickett's Charge.

In 1863 the Confederate Congress adopted the "Stainless Banner". Only one Florida unit flag of this Second National pattern is known to exist, an inscribed banner of the consolidated 1st and 4th Florida Regiment. In March 1865, the Confederate government adopted the Third National flag. One known example of this pattern is that of the 5th Florida Cavalry Battalion, inscribed with battle honors for the Battles of Olustee and Natural Bridge.

To learn more, see: "Battle Flags of Florida Troops in Confederate Service" by Daisy Parker, *Apalachee*, No. 3, 1948-1950.

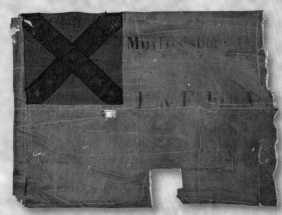

1st and 4th Florida Regiment (consolidated) flag.
(Image courtesy of the Museum of Florida History)

Fort Jefferson. *(Image courtesy of the State Archives of Florida)*

—— Monroe County ——

Garden Key

FORT JEFFERSON
Dry Tortugas National Park
305.242.7700
www.nps.gov/drto

Construction on the "Gibraltar of the Gulf," Fort Jefferson, began in 1846 at the western end of the Florida Keys to protect the Florida Straits. The largest all-masonry fort in the Western Hemisphere, construction on the fort continued for 30 years until after the advent of rifled cannon made the 8-foot thick walls obsolete. With the threat of Florida's secession from the Union in late 1860, the superintending engineer for construction at Fort Jefferson, Captain Montgomery C. Meigs, called for reinforcements to prevent its seizure by Southern militia. In response, the gunboat USS *Mohawk* was sent from Key West in November 1860 to discourage any seizure attempts. In January 1861, after Florida had seceded from the Union, a force of 66 men of the 2nd U.S. Artillery arrived at Fort Jefferson from Boston, and the fort was secured for the Union. In May 1861, Meigs was promoted to brigadier general and served as the Quartermaster General of the Union Army during the Civil War. For the remainder of the Civil War, Fort Jefferson served as an important Union military post and a military prison. At one point, it was home to some 2,000 occupants, including soldiers, their families, laborers, and prisoners. In July 1865, Fort Jefferson received its most infamous prisoners when four men convicted for conspiracy in the assassination of President Lincoln were imprisoned there, including Dr. Samuel Mudd, the Maryland physician who had set the broken leg of John Wilkes Booth. During a yellow fever outbreak in 1867, after the prison doctor died, Dr. Mudd risked his life to provide treatment to his jailers and the soldiers of the fort. Due largely in part to this life-saving service, President Andrew Johnson pardoned Mudd in 1869. As one of the most remote parks in the national parks system, Fort Jefferson is accessible only by boat and seaplane which depart from Key West, 70 miles away.

Blockade

Adapting an element of General Winfield Scott's "Anaconda Plan" for a Federal victory, President Abraham Lincoln declared a blockade of the Confederate states in April 1861. Secretary of the Navy Gideon Welles established several squadrons to blockade the Confederate coastline. Created in early 1862, the East Gulf Blockading Squadron (EGBS) had responsibility for the blockade of the Florida peninsula from Cape Canaveral on the Atlantic coast to St. Andrew Bay in the Gulf of Mexico. In northeast Florida, Fernandina became a center of operations for the South Atlantic Blockading Squadron after its capture by Union forces in March 1862. After its recapture in May 1862, the Pensacola Navy Yard served as an important depot for the West Gulf Blockading Squadron.

The EGBS captured or destroyed over 280 blockade-runners valued at more than $7 million, heavily damaged the sugar and salt-making industries along the Florida coast, provided haven for Unionist refugees and escaped slaves, conducted raids, and participated in combined operations with Union army forces. EGBS vessels were generally stationed at St. Andrew Bay, St. Joseph's Bay, Apalachicola, St. Marks, Cedar Key, Tampa Bay, Charlotte Harbor, Jupiter Inlet, and Indian River. Some also patrolled the northern coast of Cuba and the northern Bahamas. The squadron headquarters was at Key West, which was also home to the prize court where captured blockade runners were condemned and sold at auction.

To learn more, see: *Blockaders, Refugees & Contrabands: Civil War on Florida's Gulf Coast, 1861-1865* by George Buker, University of Alabama Press, 1993.

Union blockading vessels at Tampa Bay, 1864. *(Image courtesy of the State Archives of Florida)*

Key West

By the time of the Civil War, Key West was Florida's second largest city with an economy based largely on maritime activities including wrecking, or marine salvage activity, on ships wrecked on the nearby Florida Reef. Due to its strategic location astride the Caribbean and deep channels which provided protected anchorage, the United States military had maintained a presence on the island since 1822. In 1845, construction began on a massive brick fortification to protect the harbor. It was named Fort Zachary Taylor in 1850. In January 1861, after receiving word that Florida had seceded from the Union, the small U.S. Army force stationed in Key West under the command of Captain James M. Brannan moved into Fort Taylor and strengthened its defenses. Reinforcements under the command of Major William H. French arrived in March 1861, and, in May 1861, Major French placed Key West under martial law. Key West had been secured and remained in Union possession throughout the Civil War. It served as an important supply base and naval fueling depot. The headquarters of both the U.S. Navy's East Gulf Blockading Squadron and the U.S. Army's District of Key West and Tortugas were located in Key West during the war. Nearly 300 captured Confederate blockade runner ships were brought before the Key West prize court to be condemned for sale at auction. To bolster the city's defenses, construction was begun on two additional fortifications, the East and West Martello Towers, in 1862.

Confederate Secretary of State Judah P. Benjamin.
(Image courtesy of the State Archives of Florida)

End of War and Escape of Confederate Officials

The surrender of General Robert E. Lee's Army of Northern Virginia on April 9, 1865 set in motion events that led to the conflict's conclusion. News reached Florida about a week later, followed shortly by word of President Lincoln's assassination. Shocking as these events were, Lee's capitulation had not included Confederate units in Florida. Major General Sam Jones, who commanded Confederate forces in the state, initially called for continued resistance. He soon learned, however, that General Joseph E. Johnston was negotiating the surrender of his Army of Tennessee as well. The provisions of Johnston's April 26 surrender included the capitulation of Confederate troops in Florida. Union Major General James Wilson ordered Brigadier General Edward McCook of his command to proceed from Macon, Georgia to occupy Tallahassee and receive the surrender there. McCook arrived in the capital on May 10, with a final transfer of power ceremony taking place on May 20. Not until June did the final Confederates in the southern part of the peninsula capitulate.

Another aspect of the war's end was the escape of various Confederate officials who hoped to reach safety in Cuba or the Bahamas by traveling through Florida. Secretary of State Judah P. Benjamin eluded his pursuers by traveling down the Florida Gulf coast and staying at the Gamble Mansion on the Manatee River before reaching Cuba. Meanwhile another group, including Confederate Secretary of War John C. Breckinridge, likewise reached safety in Cuba. Confederate Attorney General George Davis hid out in the state for several months before attempting passage to the Bahamas in a small boat. Unsuccessful, he was forced into Key West, where he surrendered.

To learn more, see: "The Surrender of Tallahassee" by James P. Jones and William Warren Rogers, *Apalachee*, No. 6, 1963-1967. And: *Flight Into Oblivion* by Alfred Jackson Hanna, Louisiana State University Press, 1999 (reprint of 1938 edition, with forward by William C. Davis).

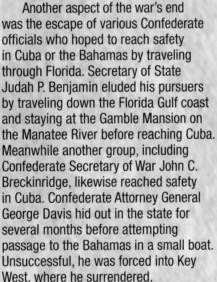

Union Brigadier General Edward M. McCook.
(Image courtesy of the State Archives of Florida)

CIVIL WAR MONUMENTS

Union Monument
Greene and Whitehead Streets

Located in Clinton Square Park, this obelisk monument was erected in 1866 by the Navy Club of Key West, in honor of the Union troops who died while stationed at Key West during the war. It is believed to be the oldest extant Civil War monument in the state, and one of the oldest in the country.

Union Yellow Fever Monument
1500 Block of Truman Avenue

Located in Bayview Park, the monument was erected by the State of New York following the Civil War, in memory of the men of the 90th and 91st New York Infantry who perished in Key West in 1862, mainly from yellow fever.

EAST AND WEST MARTELLO TOWERS

East Martello Tower
3501 South Roosevelt Boulevard
305.296.3913
www.kwahs.com/martello.htm

West Martello Tower
1100 Atlantic Boulevard
305.294.3210
www.keywestgardenclub.com

In 1862, the Union military began construction on two fortifications, known as the East and West Martello Towers, on the south shore of Key West

Fort Zachary Taylor, Key West. *(Image courtesy of the Florida Park Service)*

to provide defensive support to Fort Zachary Taylor. The West Martello Tower was built about one and one-half miles east of Fort Taylor, and the East Martello Tower is located two miles east of the West Tower. Construction continued throughout the Civil War years. The masonry work was substantially completed by the end of the war, but the outer works were never finished and no armament was installed. The wartime development of rifled artillery rendered such masonry fortifications obsolete, and by 1866 construction of the original plans was suspended. In 1947, the structures were declared surplus by the U.S. Army and sold to Monroe County, which later leased East Martello to the Key West Art & Historical Society and West Martello to the Key West Garden Club. East Martello is operated as a museum with a large collection of Key West artifacts, historical records, and military memorabilia including Civil War objects. At West Martello, a permanent horticultural exhibit on the grounds is maintained by the Garden Club. Of the two fortifications, the East Martello Tower has retained more of its Civil War appearance and has essentially survived in the form of its original construction, while the West Martello Tower was

modified by the military during the Spanish American War and later periods.

FORT ZACHARY TAYLOR HISTORIC STATE PARK
Southard Street
305.292.6713
www.floridastateparks.org/forttaylor
www.forttaylor.org

Sited to protect the strategic harbor at Key West, construction of Fort Zachary Taylor began in 1845 some 1,200 feet offshore from the city. After Florida seceded from the Union in January 1861, U.S. Army Captain James Brannan moved his troops from the city into the fort to prevent its seizure by Florida militia. For the remainder of the war, Fort Taylor served as an important Union military post, and by 1865 was armed with approximately 150 cannons of varying sizes. Fort Taylor continued in service as an army post until 1947 when it was decommissioned by the U.S. Army, and was then utilized by the U.S. Navy as a storage facility. In the mid 1960's, the U.S. Navy deposited dredging fill at the fort, connecting it to the mainland. In 1968, excavations of the casements unearthed many of the original armaments from the fort. Recovered

items included numerous cannons, gun cradles, carriages, a desalinization plant, and more than 1,000 cannonballs and projectiles. Today, Fort Taylor is considered to have the largest collection of Civil War era cannons in the United States, with others still buried in the casements. In 1976, the U.S. Department of the Interior transferred Fort Taylor to the State of Florida for use as a state park facility. The park is the site of the annual Key West Civil War Heritage Days festival in February, with Confederate and Union reenactors participating in public events and activities, including a sea battle with schooners.

HEMINGWAY HOUSE
907 Whitehead Street
305.294.1136
www.hemingwayhome.com

Constructed in c.1850, this house was the residence of prosperous businessman Asa F. Tift, a delegate to the Florida Secession Convention who fled to Georgia after the occupation of Key West by Union forces in 1861. With his brother Nelson Tift of Albany, Georgia, Asa Tift designed and financed the construction of Confederate ironclads during the Civil War including the CSS *Mississippi* at New Orleans and the CSS *Atlanta* at Savannah, Georgia.

KEY WEST CEMETERY

701 Passover Lane
305.292.8177
www.keywestcity.com/egov/
docs/1158849616888.htm

Founded in 1847, this cemetery contains the remains of numerous Civil War army and navy veterans, both Confederate and Union, with many buried in special veterans sections. Among the Confederate veterans buried here is Captain Henry Mulrennan who commanded "The Key West Avengers", a company formed from men who fled Union-held Key West. The unit first served in the Confederate Coast Guard at Tampa and later in the 7th Florida Infantry in the western theater. After being captured and held in a Union prison camp in New York, Mulrennan returned to Key West and was elected mayor in the postwar period.

KEY WEST LIGHTHOUSE

938 Whitehead Street
305.294.0012
www.kwahs.com/lighthouse.htm

The present Key West Lighthouse was constructed in 1847 to replace the earlier 1825 lighthouse destroyed by the hurricane of 1846, and was an important navigational aid during the Civil War. Due to the quick action of Union forces in securing Key West, the lighthouse did not go dark in 1861 as most Florida lighthouses did, although the 79-year-old lighthouse keeper, Barbara Mabrity, was suspected of being a Confederate sympathizer. In 1864, the 82-year-old Mabrity was removed from her job, after she refused to retire, for being disloyal to the Union. She had held the position since 1832 when she replaced her husband as keeper when he died. The lighthouse and the adjacent 1886 lighthouse keeper's quarters are now operated as a museum by the Key West Art & Historical Society.

"KEY WEST OLDEST HOUSE"

322 Duval Street
305.294.9501
www.oirf.org/museum.htm

Constructed in c.1829 and moved to its current location in c.1836, this house was the residence of Francis Watlington, who served as a lieutenant in the Confederate

Navy Squadron at Mobile, Alabama, including service on the gunboat CSS *Gaines* and the ironclad ram CSS *Tennessee*. He surrendered and was paroled in May 1865.

MALLORY HOMESITE HISTORICAL MARKER

Front and Whitehead Streets

Located in Clinton Square Park, this marker was erected by the Historical Association of Southern Florida near the site of where the Mallory family home stood from 1839 to 1895. Stephen R. Mallory was serving as United States Senator when Florida seceded from the Union in 1861. He resigned his Senate seat and was appointed Confederate Secretary of the Navy, a position he held until the end of the war. His son, Stephen R. Mallory, Jr., was raised in the house and later owned it. During the

Civil War, Mallory, Jr. served in both the Confederate army and navy. The property was acquired by the U.S. Navy in 1895.

NAVAL BASE KEY WEST

The U.S. Navy first established a naval base at Key West in 1823 for the suppression of piracy in the Caribbean Sea and the Gulf of Mexico. During the Civil War, Key West was the headquarters of the U.S. Navy's East Gulf Blockading Squadron, which had responsibility for the blockade of the Florida peninsula from Cape Canaveral on the Atlantic coast to St. Andrew Bay in the Gulf of Mexico. Surviving buildings used by the Union navy during the Civil War include:

United States Marine Hospital
401 Emma Street

Designed by Robert Mills, designer of the Washington Monument, this building was constructed in 1845 and was used for treatment of Union military personnel

Stephen Mallory

Stephen Mallory of Key West served as Confederate Secretary of Navy from 1861 until 1865, the only individual to serve in the same cabinet position throughout the existence of the Confederacy. A U.S. Senator before the war, Mallory promoted the establishment of a naval base at Key West, introduced bills to construct maritime hospitals at several Florida locations, and supported the construction of new warships. Mallory supported secession, but hoped to avoid war. Before resigning his senate seat in January 1861, he helped negotiate a truce between U.S. and Southern forces at Pensacola. He returned to Florida, but the following month Confederate President Jefferson Davis selected him as Secretary of the Navy.

Aware that the Confederacy could not match the Union navy ship for ship, Mallory promoted the use of commerce raiders and ironclad vessels, as well as submarines, underwater mines, and heavy rifled cannon. At war's end, Mallory evacuated Richmond with President Davis, remaining with the

Confederate Secretary of Navy Stephen Mallory.
(Image courtesy of the State Archives of Florida)

president's party until early May 1865, when he resigned to return to Florida. He was imprisoned by Federal authorities until March 1866. Subsequently he practiced law in Pensacola, never again holding public office. He died in 1873.

To learn more, see: *Stephen Russell Mallory, A Biography of the Confederate Navy Secretary and United States Senator* by Rodman L. Underwood, McFarland & Company, 2005.

including victims of the yellow fever epidemics which swept Key West during the Civil War.

Clinton Square Market
291 Front Street

Constructed in 1856-1861, this building was used by the Union navy as a coal depot and storehouse for its vessels on blockading duty.

— Palm Beach County —

Jupiter

JUPITER INLET LIGHTHOUSE
500 Captain Armour's Way
561.747.8380
www.lrhs.org

The Jupiter Inlet Lighthouse is the oldest surviving structure in Palm Beach County. Designed by then-Lieutenant George Gordon Meade, who would later command the Union Army at the Battle of Gettysburg, it was completed and lit on July 10, 1860, after a six year construction period. Determining the light to be of use to Union ships and a detriment to their cause, Confederate sympathizers took control of the lighthouse in August 1861. They removed lamps and burners from the light, and buried the equipment. Throughout most of the war, Jupiter Inlet was an active area for Confederate blockade running and, by the end of the war, Union blockading ships had captured or sunk over 50 Confederate boats in and around the inlet. The Union navy also sent numerous raiding expeditions into the area. In the summer of 1862, Union sailors landed and broke into the Jupiter Inlet Lighthouse and confiscated journals and other lighthouse records. In February 1863, another Union raiding force uncovered the hidden lighthouse apparatus and brought it to Key West, but the lighthouse remained darkened for the duration of the war. The Jupiter Inlet Light returned to operation in June 1866. The lighthouse is now part of the Jupiter Inlet Lighthouse and Museum complex operated by the Loxahatchee River Historical Society. Located in a restored World War II barracks building, the museum contains exhibits on local history, including the Civil War.

West Palm Beach

WOODLAWN CEMETERY
U.S. Highway 1

In a roundabout at its center, this cemetery contains a Confederate monument erected by the United Daughters of the Confederacy in 1941. Also buried in this cemetery are approximately 30 Union veterans, including Willmon Whilldin of the 6th New Jersey Infantry who was mayor of West Palm Beach in the postwar period.

Pensions

In 1885, the Florida legislature passed one of the first true pension laws in the South, authorizing payments to Confederate veterans unfit to work as a result of wounds. An 1887 revision authorized pensions to current state residents who had served in units from other Confederate states, greatly increasing the number of pensioners. The legislature next authorized pensions to the widows of veterans who had been killed or died of wounds. Eventually, pension rules permitted widows who had married their husbands decades after the war to receive pensions. By 1910, Florida had 5,905 veterans and widows on its pension rolls, and paid out $644,606 in benefits.

The last surviving veteran pensioner was William A. Lundy, who claimed service in the Alabama Home Guard. During the last years of his life, Lundy reached celebrity status as one of the last Confederate veterans, although recent research casts strong doubt on his service claim. His death in 1957 ended 72 years of benefits to Confederate soldiers. The number of widows dwindled until April 1985, when Nena Feagle of Columbia County died, marking the end of a century of welfare provided by Florida to Civil War veterans and widows.

To learn more, see: "Florida Confederate Pension Application Files," State Library & Archives of Florida. Available online at: http://www.floridamemory.com/collections/pensionfiles

Florida Confederate Widow's Pension Claim, 1909.
(Image courtesy of the State Archives of Florida)

Florida Monument, Chickamauga Battlefield, Georgia. *(Image courtesy of the National Park Service)*

GEORGIA

FLORIDA MONUMENT, CHICKAMAUGA

LaFayette Road
Chickamauga & Chattanooga National Military Park
706.866.9241
www.nps.gov/chch

Fought on September 19-20, 1863, the Battle of Chickamauga was one of the bloodiest battles of the Civil War, with nearly 35,000 Union and Confederate casualties. Seven Florida units participated in the battle and suffered over 550 dead, wounded, missing or captured. The large Florida Monument at the battlefield was constructed in 1912-1913, and was dedicated in May 1913 during the twenty-third National United Confederate Veterans Reunion held at nearby Chattanooga, Tennessee.

MISSISSIPPI

FLORIDA MONUMENT, VICKSBURG

South Confederate Avenue
Vicksburg National Military Park
601.636.0583
www.nps.gov/vick/historyculture/florida-memorial.htm

Erected by the Florida Division of the United Daughters of the Confederacy

in 1954, the Florida Monument is located on former national park property which was later deeded back to the City of Vicksburg. This granite monolith monument commemorates the service of the three Florida regiments in General Joseph E. Johnston's Army of Relief which was unable to break the Union siege of Vicksburg in 1863.

PENNSYLVANIA

FLORIDA MONUMENT, GETTYSBURG

West Confederate Avenue
Gettysburg National Military Park
717.334.1124
www.nps.gov/gett

At the Battle of Gettysburg, the Florida Brigade (comprised of the 2nd, 5th, and 8th Florida Infantry Regiments), under the command of Colonel David Lang, participated in the heaviest fighting of July 2 and 3, 1863, including an advance in support of Pickett's Charge. The monument states that of the 700 men in the Florida Brigade, 445 were killed, wounded, or captured. A more recent study concludes that the Florida Brigade started with 739 men and suffered 343 casualties. Either way, the Florida Brigade suffered among the highest percentage of casualties of any

Florida Monument, Gettysburg Battlefield, Pennsylvania. *(Image courtesy of the State Archives of Florida)*

Confederate brigade at Gettysburg. The Florida Monument was dedicated on July 3, 1963; the 100th anniversary of the Florida Brigade's assault to assist Pickett's Charge. An iron marker with information on the Florida Brigade at the Battle of Gettysburg was erected on West Confederate Avenue in 1902 by the Gettysburg National Military Park Commission, and then replaced with a larger bronze marker in 1910. A second Florida Brigade iron marker was erected by the Commission on Emmitsburg Road.

TENNESSEE

FLORIDA MONUMENT, FRANKLIN

1345 Carnton Lane
McGavock Confederate Cemetery
615.794.0903
http://carnton.org

Maintained by the United Daughters of the Confederacy, the McGavock Confederate Cemetery is believed to be the largest privately held Confederate cemetery in the United States. It contains the remains of nearly 1,500 Confederate casualties from the November 1864 Battle of Franklin, buried by state, including members of the Florida Brigade. The Florida section contains a monument and 4 gravesites. Approximately 5-foot tall, the Florida shaft monument was erected in the late 19th century.

VIRGINIA

FLORIDA MONUMENT, WINCHESTER

305 East Boscawen Street
Mount Hebron Cemetery
540.662.4868
www.mthebroncemetery.org/stonewall.html

Located in the Stonewall Confederate Cemetery section of the Mount Hebron Cemetery, the Florida plot contains an obelisk monument in front of the marked graves of 38 Florida Confederate soldiers. It was erected in 1902 by the Florida Division of the United Daughters of the Confederacy.

SELECTED BIBLIOGRAPHY

Printed Resources

Brown, Canter Jr.
Tampa in Civil War and Reconstruction.
Tampa, FL: University of Tampa Press, 2000.

Buker, George.
Blockaders, Refugees & Contrabands: Civil War on Florida's Gulf Coast, 1861-1865.
Tuscaloosa, AL: University of Alabama Press, 1993.

Davis, William W.
The Civil War and Reconstruction in Florida.
1913. Reprint edition. Gainesville, FL: University of Florida Press, 1964.

Dickison, Mary Elizabeth.
Dickison and His Men: Reminiscences of the War in Florida.
1890. Reprint edition. Gainesville, FL: University of Florida Press, 1962.

Driscoll, John K.
The Civil War on Pensacola Bay, 1861-1862.
Jefferson, NC: McFarland & Company, Inc., 2007.

Florida Humanities Council.
The Civil War: When Florida "Opened Up the Gates of Hell." Special Issue of *Forum: The Magazine of the Florida Humanities Council.* Volume 34, Number 1, Spring 2010.

Hartman, David W.
and David J. Coles, compilers.
Biographical Rosters of Florida's Confederate and Union Soldiers, 1861-1865.
Wilmington, N.C.: Broadfoot Publishing Company, 1995.

Holland, Keith V., Lee Manley, and James W. Towart, editors.
The Maple Leaf: An Extraordinary Civil War Shipwreck.
Jacksonville, FL: St. Johns Archaeological Expeditions, Inc., 1993.

Johns, John E.
Florida During the Civil War.
Gainesville, FL: University of Florida Press, 1963.

Martin, Richard A., and Daniel L. Schafer.
Jacksonville's Ordeal by Fire: A Civil War History.
Jacksonville, FL: Florida Publishing Company, 1984.

Nulty, William H.
Confederate Florida: The Road to Olustee.
Tuscaloosa, AL: University of Alabama Press, 1990.

Pearce, George F.
Pensacola During the Civil War: A Thorn in the Side of the Confederacy.
Gainesville, FL: University Press of Florida, 2000.

Proctor, Samuel, editor.
Florida a Hundred Years Ago.
Tallahassee, FL: Florida State Library, 1960-1965. (Day by day listing of events in Civil War Florida.)

Revels, Tracy J.
Grander in Her Daughters: Florida's Women During the Civil War.
Columbia, SC: University of South Carolina Press, 2004.

Rivers, Larry Eugene.
Slavery in Florida: Territorial Days to Emancipation.
Gainesville, FL: University Press of Florida, 2000.

Schafer, Daniel L.
Thunder on the River: The Civil War in Northeast Florida.
Gainesville, FL: University Press of Florida, 2010.

Schmidt, Lewis G.
The Civil War in Florida: A Military History.
4 vols. in 6 pts. Allentown, PA: Published by the author, 1989-1992.

Shofner, Jerrell H.
Nor Is It Over Yet: Florida in the Era of Reconstruction, 1863-1877.
Gainesville, FL: University Press of Florida, 1974.

Soldiers of Florida in the Seminole Indian, Civil and Spanish-American Wars. Prepared and published under the auspices of the Board of State Institutions, 1903. Reprint edition. Macclenny, FL: Richard J. Ferry, 1983.

Taylor, Paul, editor.
Discovering the Civil War in Florida: A Reader and Guide.
Sarasota, FL: Pineapple Press, Inc., 2001.

Taylor, Robert A.
Rebel Storehouse: Florida in the Confederate Economy.
Tuscaloosa, AL: University of Alabama Press, 1995.

Winsboro, Irvin D. S., editor.
Florida's Civil War: Explorations into Conflict, Interpretations and Memory.
Cocoa, FL: The Florida Historical Society Press, 2007.

Wynne, Lewis N. and Robert A. Taylor.
Florida in the Civil War.
Charleston, SC: Arcadia Publishing, 2001.

Please see sidebars
for additional printed sources.

Internet Web Sites

A Guide to Civil War Records at the State Archives of Florida
www.floridamemory.com/collections/civilwarguide

Civil War Florida
Jim Studnicki, Webmaster
www.civilwarflorida.com

Destination: Civil War
Florida Public Archaeology Network
www.flpublicarchaeology.org/civilwar

Florida in the Civil War
State Library & Archives of Florida
www.floridamemory.com/onlineclassroom/floridacivilwar

Florida in the Civil War, 1861-1865
Museum of Florida History
www.museumoffloridahistory.com/exhibits/permanent/civilwar

The Civil War in Florida
Dale Cox, Author
www.exploresouthernhistory.com/cwflorida.html

This Day in Florida History: Civil War, 1861-1865
Florida Historical Society
www.myfloridahistory.org/library/flahistory/civilwar

INDEX

INDEX
(continued)

Index note: A number of these sites have components that could be listed under more than one heading. For simplicity, sites are listed once under their primary feature.

ACKNOWLEDGEMENTS

Artifact Photography
Ray Stanyard

**Bagdad Village
Preservation Association**
Michael Johnson

City of Orlando
Richard Forbes
Donald Price

Florida Association of Museums
Malinda Horton

**Florida Division of
Historical Resources**
David Ferro
Sharyn Heiland
Susanne Hunt
Marie C. Ivory

Florida Division of State Lands
Dr. Joe Knetsch

Florida Historic Capitol
Andrew Edel

Florida Park Service
Ellen Andrews
Mark Knapke
Martha Robinson
Phillip Werndli

Florida Public Archaeology Network
Dr. William Lees

Florida Supreme Court Library
Erik Robinson

Manatee County Historical Commission
Joe Kennedy
Cathy Slusser

Marine Archaeological Council
Steven Singer

Museum of Florida History
Bruce Graetz
Kieran Orr

Orange County Regional History Center
Jeff Grzelak

Reflections of Manatee
Trudy Williams

Research Historian
Sidney Johnston

State Archives of Florida
Dr. R. Boyd Murphree
N. Adam Watson

St. Augustine Historical Society
Charles Tingley

St. Augustine Lighthouse & Museum
Kathy Fleming

St. Cloud Heritage Museum
Roger Heiple

Treasures of Madison County
William Bunting, Sr.

United Daughters of the Confederacy
Patricia Schnurr

Wakulla County Historical Society
Dr. Madeleine Hirsiger-Carr